T0102519

– IN THE MOMENT –

Permaculture

Planting the Seeds of Radical Regeneration

Maya Blackwell

Saraband

Published by Saraband
3 Clairmont Gardens
Glasgow, G3 7LW

www.saraband.net

ISBN: 9781913393830

Printed and bound in Great Britain by Clays Ltd, Elcograf S.p.A.

1 2 3 4 5 6 7 8 9 10

Contents

Prologue 1
How to Use this Book 9
What Is Permaculture? 11
Why Is it Important? 26
The Twelve Design Principles 37

EARTH CARE
The Design Process 62
Soil 77
Water 91
Plants 99
Animals 114

PEOPLE CARE
Self Care 126
Group Work 143
Wide-Scale People Care 155

FAIR SHARE
Intersectional Permaculture 180
Urban Permaculture 197
Restorative Activism 212

Epilogue 231
How to Get Involved 233
Bibliography 241
Endnotes 243
Acknowledgments 263

For Dan Sterling,

you are my marrow, my heart,
my every good intention.

Thank you for making the world feel like
a place worth fighting for.

Prologue

Permaculture found me at age twenty, utterly baffled by the state of the world. I phrase it this way because when we step onto a path that ignites passion or purpose, it is as if a force is intentionally seeking us out. Life can be cataclysmic and chaotic; we are mostly fumbling through each moment, attempting to find a centre amongst it all. Well, I am at least. It is rare to be able to pin our finger to a moment and see how it has sprawled out into each fibril of our life. But there is something mystical in imagining an omnipotent being, some all-knowing string-puller, picking me out in my sea of confusion and angst and placing me in the arms of my life.

* * *

I had gone through the motions of navigating youth in the Western world. I had moved through the education system with force-fed notions of making it as an individual. I was sold the capitalist story of growth. Not the kind of growth that trees embody: slow, sturdy, patient, but the kind of growth that is killing the planet. The kind of growth that tells us to find what we are, find it now, and then find some way for it to make us money.

After leaving school, I embarked on the modern incarnation of pilgrimage: a 'gap year' through Europe and the Himalayas, hoping that if I travelled overseas I'd somehow find myself. As if 'myself' was something happening in the Big Out There, not the husk of flesh I walk around in each day.

I had very much intended to look out of train windows in the rain and have profound realisations, with all of the self-indulgent melancholy you might expect from a young adult who writes poetry. Instead, I cried a lot and missed my mum. I looked out of train windows with apt longing, surprised to find only myself staring back at me.

When I returned to Devon, England, where I grew up, I was lacking in a sense of direction. To put it more frankly, I was absolutely shitting myself.

It's an odd dichotomy to reckon with as a young person, or any person really: the dominant narrative tells us that happiness is obtained through accumulating wealth and consuming as much as possible. But there is also the knowledge that we are living on this planet by utilising finite resources, acting as if we have infinity at our fingertips. I was exhausted by the pressure of pretending this didn't terrify me.

I grew up in a forest. I was part of a New Age traveller community and spent the first sixteen years of my life living in a double-decker bus. My parents had decided to live this way from the same place I write these words: an inherent dissatisfaction with living in a system that exploits our bodies for the profit of faceless invisible forces. I assume some initial thoughts arise when hearing about this type of community. Maybe it conjures up images of crusty jugglers and freegans, wafty hippies singing 'Kumbaya' by firelight, preaching about harmony with nature whilst wasting away their parents' trust funds. Don't get me wrong, that was part of it.

But in this community, you could also find my mother. She's a robust woman, insecure and wounded, but a survivor. Her bones are strong as nettle twine, unbreakable and unwavering. She is soft but hardened, like many women of her generation who were given far less opportunity than me to find their voice in the world. The 'Mother' or 'Demeter' archetype arises throughout various forms of mythology and folklore. In paganism, it depicts the divine feminine. In Greek Mythology, Demeter is the goddess of agriculture and harvest.[1] In essence, permaculture calls upon this spirit that we associate with mothers but lives inside all of us: a deep sense of stewardship of our kin. Not just fellow human beings but all beings that we coexist with. It is this sense of responsibility to bestow all the riches of a healthy planet to our future children that lives at the heart of permaculture.

I spent the majority of the time I lived there resenting my way of life. I attended a Christian school in the local village and was bullied ruthlessly for living the way I lived, so my rebellion was not what you'd usually expect from a teenager. Instead, I worked hard in school, found solace in books, and decided I wanted a proper adult job; I wanted the nuclear family dream; I wanted a clean life. The irony is not lost on me that after years of this searching, I found myself back where I started. Angry at the system that had created me, wanting to escape from the pressures of it all and live amongst the trees.

All I had was a hungry heart, an appetite to activate my fear and transmute it into hope. I knew I liked to sit beneath the trees, I liked the sense of belonging I embodied when doing so. I knew I was scared for the future of the planet. I knew I wanted to plant seeds and watch them grow. But I had none of the skills or resources to do so, just a sense that I wanted the world to be different. I longed to belong to a forest of hope, a community of folk who planted trees and sat beneath them together. I was also grieving my first love. It was my first encounter with the beast of heartache and I was absolutely distraught.

I moved to Bristol, a city just two hours from where I was born. After traipsing the globe to find elusive meaning, I was confronted with the reality that I only wanted to find a home in myself. To belong to something that mattered. I applied for Shift Bristol, a Practical Sustainability course. I barely looked at the course guide; I just leapt into it, hoping to find that belonging. And it found me.

Permaculture in its simplest form is a low-impact land management approach that works holistically, embodying nature's slow and cyclical processes.[2] It is also something far deeper and sacred than that if you allow yourself to be led by it. Part of permaculture is to look for patterns, to pay attention to the subtle ways nature shows us that the details of our lives that may appear separate are, in fact, interwoven into the fabric of all life. The opportunity to write this book coincided with a second heartbreak. There is something profound about how permaculture has found me again, grief-stricken, and asked me to dive deeper into my curiosity and connection to nature and to reacquaint myself with the community that taught me how to heal. It seems preferable to ugly crying to the same three Joni Mitchell songs and scrolling through my ex's Facebook pictures, at the very least.

When I lost one of my closest friends to suicide, a tree was planted in his memory. My friends and I gather at that elm on occasion, noticing how it has grown in his absence. We greet that with appropriate sorrow and awe. His name was Dan Sterling. I write his name often, wherever I can. In the years since he left us, I have scribbled his initials into muddy car windows, sand grains, and snow. You will find his name woven throughout the pages of this book. I like the feeling that the lessons I learned from him can be passed on to others. It is the beauty of storytelling: that no one can ever truly be gone as long as the story keeps being written. He is a reminder of what is possible, of how we can activate hope from the deepest depths of our suffering, and how we can plant trees there.

I write about this loss because it is something we can all relate to as human beings. It is eventual, inevitable, and brutal. I lost Dan amid a global pandemic where disconnection was on the rise and we felt more alone than ever. But such monumental grief brought me and my community together. It seems paradoxical that loss can bind us, but such is the symbiosis of Earth, the perennial give and take of life and death.

Loss is also the place from which permaculture was born. This design methodology arrived as a response to the modern, industrial world's destruction of the environment.[3] I assume, in some ways, loss brought you here, reading these words. Some sense that the world we live in does not serve us, and some yearning to find a simpler and slower way of life, one which is harmonious with nature rather than exploitative. One which no longer separates us from the trees.

This book will guide you through the principles of permaculture, and how you can use them when working with the land. But beyond that, there is another invitation extended to you. To dig a little deeper into your wild and weird soils. To plant seedlings of dreams and hopes where there may be fear and disillusionment. With each chapter, there will be opportunities to learn how to view the world around you through the lens of permaculture and how to integrate these skills into your environment, whatever that may be. Maybe not all of it will apply to you because access to land is more restricted than ever.[4] The elite disproportionately owns land; over half of the land in England is owned by 1% of the population, so it is off limits and unaffordable for the vast majority of us.[5] But you don't need to have expanses of land for permaculture to work for you. Everything you read here is adaptable to your circumstance. Permaculture is intrinsically versatile, built to be resilient to change. Just like our planet.

Alongside learning a design process, there is an invitation here to return to yourself, to enliven that which may feel lost. There will be offerings throughout this book to reconnect to your warm body, to your beating heart, to commit to that glorious and frightening act of paying attention. My greatest hope, if you'll let me share it, is that you may find belonging in these pages. Whether that's belonging to yourself, to the land, or to a community; it is all the same regardless.

The fire is stoked, the kettle is on the hob and the door is on the latch. Make yourself at home.

Chapter 1
How to Use this Book

This book is an invitation to learn the basics of permaculture and connect more intimately to the world you inhabit, internally and externally. Permaculture design is a site-specific process because we focus our attention on our local land by working with the resources and wildlife already available to us. This means that alongside this book, you will likely have to do your own research, in order to apply what is offered here to your unique context. This is the joy of intentional gardening work – the more we remain curious and committed to learning, the more intimate and insightful our conversations with the natural world become. I will provide you with an outline of what permaculture is in practice and what it means for us as people on a personal and global level.

I am also an arts and health facilitator. This means I value art and creativity and believe they have the power to improve our health, well-being and connection to the Earth. Tending to grief is another core facet of my work, so there will be explorations around this topic. This book contains invitations for reflective and creative mindfulness and nature connection activities. I hope that through engaging with these activities, you can take away practical ways to bind creativity and nature connection with growing and planting in your everyday life. Creativity is essential to permaculture design because you learn how to get the most out of what you implement, adapt to situations, and develop resilient and innovative solutions.

I recommend keeping a journal alongside this book, so you can write down anything you learn and have a space to practise the creative activities outlined here. It will also come in handy when creating your permaculture system.

The invitations will reflect the learning process, allowing you to embed knowledge while connecting more deeply to yourself and nature. There will also be questions throughout this book, which are intended to spark curiosity and bring the themes and concepts explored back to your personal experience, your big heart, your soul body. Permaculture is an intentional and ever-changing practice, so we learn from this most usefully when we relate it back to ourselves as individuals. These are not infallible concepts, they are active practices that we can put forth into the world to try and make it better. Where there are prompts for reflection, I invite you to respond in whatever way you feel compelled to. Claim your own space and take your sweet time. This book, like nature, is not in a hurry.

Chapter 2

What Is Permaculture?

'Blessed are old people who plant trees knowing that they shall never sit in the shade of their foliage.'[1]

Permaculture could be described as a practice of returning. Bill Mollison and David Holmgren coined the term in the late seventies, an amalgamation of *permanent* and *agriculture*. It is a design methodology detailing how to create harmonious human settlements rather than exploitative ones.[2] A whole-system approach achieves this through guiding principles, a deep respect for nature, and a willingness to try, fail and adapt.[3] At the heart of permaculture are two essential governing forces: a commitment to observation over time and Indigenous knowledge.[4]

Permaculture tells us that the most radical form of opposition against the destruction of our planet is the creation of localised, autonomous systems that replace high-energy, polluting industrial technologies with more considered biological resources.[5] It is a slow, gentle revolution. Its defiance is potent; it stands strong against industrial power, and it blooms.

A permaculture system includes high biodiversity and on-site water management and energy systems, and it focuses on a thoughtful interplay of species, alongside obtaining a yield for the people creating the system.[6] This is an intentional antithesis to modernised agriculture that exploits land for monocultures and plants only for a singular function, usually intensively. Permaculture requires intentional design, observing the inputs and outputs of all that exists within our system, paying attention to the myriad values and uses each plant and animal has to offer.[7] In doing so, respect becomes an essential ingredient of the work, as we no longer reduce the land and its inhabitants to their ability to serve human beings.

There are three pillars of permaculture, how it's practised and what it means in the wider view of the world. These guiding ethics illustrate that permaculture isn't simply about land management. It is also concerned with shifting our view of the world from a capitalist, consumerist framework; it is a way of looking at any area of our lives with compassion, community and creativity at the core. It is an invitation to shift perspective, to cock our heads and try looking from a different angle.

EARTH CARE refers to how we can design regenerative land systems for the planet and, on a personal level, how we can adapt our behaviours to lessen our negative impact on the Earth. PEOPLE CARE begins with the individual: how can we take care of ourselves while simultaneously taking care of the Earth? As it expands outwardly, it looks at how we can collectivise in the face of these challenges to form networks that strengthen our ability to care for the planet whilst caring for each other. FAIR SHARE refers to how we take what we need and give to others where we can. It's about adopting a different lens and reframing what 'yield' means. Rather than focusing solely on our individual needs, fair share considers how we could be of benefit to others within our communities.[8]

To practise the art of returning, you will need nothing but observation and curiosity in your toolbox. Through the careful implementation of these skills, you can start to expand your view and widen your scope of the natural world. Nothing that exists is ever immortal. No matter how ornate in gold or successful at business, we all return to the soil. The capitalist myth we have all been buying into as a society is that nature begins and ends with us, as if we have completed some elaborate game show, won the bounty, and completed the maze. As if nature is a thing for us to win or lose. We live under the illusion that we have somehow tricked the grim reaper, that we won't return to the soil just as the blackbird and the dandelion do.

As you weave your way through these words and begin to acquaint yourself with this practice, contemplate this: what if, when we planted an apple tree, it wasn't just so we could eat as many apples as we wanted or to create shade to read under? What if we planted a tree for the sake of simply knowing the good that tree might do? For the bee who slurps a sugary sip, for the critters that feast on the fruit carcass, for the robin's afternoon snack. What if we planted the tree and envisioned our children's children feasting on the fruit?

Of course, we are, in our flesh bodies, with our names and job titles, impermanent. We will be compost in no time, so why create systems of permanence? In answering this question, we must widen our view of time and our place within it. We shift our perspective from being 'separate' from all other life: from the flora and the fauna that will exist within our system; from the children who will one day eat our apples. When we view ourselves as just another fibre in the spider's web of all existence, we may believe our job to be that of sustaining the web, not merely ourselves.

When I lost Dan, I felt, for the first time, like a thread in the spool of that web. In mainstream Western culture, we have little space to put our grief when someone dies. It's time to dust off that stiff upper lip, make finger sandwiches, wear black, and move through it stoically. I was struck by my lack of preparation for something so definitive, by the epiphany that death is actually real. I thought it was so strange, but loss shook me into a more abundant aliveness. And not in the sense you might expect. I didn't want to live each moment like it was my last, say yes to everything and transform my life from its mundanity to something 'exciting' like becoming a trapeze-artist-astronaut. Instead of changing something external or rewriting my story so I would sound impressive, should my diary be found in fifty years, I intended to take it all in; all the weedy chaos. I wanted to sink deeper into the all-encompassing nowness. I wanted to entangle myself in the vines of this life, to befriend the cavernous underbelly, the beast lurking in the dark. I wanted to kiss death on its cheek and thank it for defining life. I set out to do something as simple as planting a tree, making a salad, or drinking a cuppa and to do so in full attendance of my beating heart. It doesn't happen often, mind: I spend much of my time idly thumb-twiddling and staring at the cobwebs of my ceiling. But some days, the light catches the swooning dust in the air, or I witness new lovers in the liminal dusk, sharing private giggles and appearing utterly invincible, and I feel unequivocally tethered to life. Now that I have truly accepted that someday I will be at one with soil, my purpose – if I can be so indulgent and grandiose to assume I have one – is to befriend it.

This sense of our evanescence and deep admiration for the natural world are notions that govern the practice of permaculture and originate from the Indigenous people of Australia, as Bill Mollison worked closely with these communities living in Tasmania. The heart of permaculture is in Indigenous science; its relational essence is the core principle which brings it into being.[9]

Shawn Wilson postulates that including Indigenous views within our research requires a shift away from the modern myopic lens through which we ingest information. He writes, 'Knowledge is shared with all of creation. It is not just interpersonal relationships, not just with the research subjects I may be working with, but it's a relationship with all of creation. It is with the cosmos, it is with the animals, with the plants, with the Earth that we share this knowledge. It goes beyond the idea of individual knowledge to the concept of relational knowledge.'[10] So, when working with Indigenous communities, one must conceptualise the intentions and impact. The Western neoliberal view is one of individualism, monocultures and of a single and extracted focus. When research exists within an Indigenous paradigm, it becomes something which exists as a wider whole as opposed to individual elements analysed separately.[11]

This was the case with the emergence of permaculture, a reimagining of land management inspired by Indigenous communities and applied to the framework of our modern world. When considering Mollinson's research alongside the native people of Tasmania, there are relational benefits: it has ultimately contributed to a positive influence on our planet, it has collectivised communities and inspired people to connect more spiritually to the Earth. But how do we work to make sure our actions are relationally beneficial for the communities from which they were learned? As we develop ourselves as permaculturists, it is our responsibility to ask ourselves this question continually.

As I try to answer it, I feel clumsy and inadequate. I picture myself planted atop two tectonic plates starting to crack. As one leg moves in one direction, the other moves the opposite way, and my legs slowly start to split apart. (And trust me, I am really not flexible enough to manage the splits; I'm more of a 'lie in child's pose and try not to relive the most tragic and embarrassing moments of my life' sort of girl. But I digress.) There is value in looking critically at permaculture. As culture evolves and we become more aware of the disparities blighting our world, it's important to look at the past to do better now and in the future. However, if we do so too harshly, we risk divisiveness within a community with a shared purpose and goal, which ultimately has good intentions at its core.

Even though Mollinson and Holgrem themselves framed permaculture as an autonomous practice and referenced the influence of Indigeneity, they are now regarded as the forefathers of permaculture. This itself is problematic. It is, however, a product of the culture we exist in, one which loves to worship and revere the individual, especially when they are white men. It's a tale as old as time – or at least our modern view of time – that behind the innovations and inventions of celebrated science men, there are voices appropriated and there are people silenced. I write this and a familiar itch arises in my throat, as I try to consider the weight of such silence, the absence of such crucial voices, and the reality of how much Earth-nurturing wisdom has been erased due to violence against indigenous communities.

Bruce Pascoe writes about the history of Indigenous Australia and the ways in which his people were wrongly regarded as hunter-gatherers. They were, in fact, custodians of the most longstanding remaining culture who were actively engaged with their local land. When colonialist 'discoverers' arrived in Australia, they misinterpreted this as wild and uncultivated land. Pascoe points out that specific practices such as tilling, terracing, perennial plantations and storage and preserves were all indicators that Indigenous Australians and Torres Strait Islanders were in fact the 'original farmers'.[12] Dr Lyla June Johnston, an Indigenous musician, scholar, and community organiser of Diné (Navajo), Tsétsêhéstâhese (Cheyenne) and European lineages, also challenges this misconception of Indigenous peoples: 'Contrary to the myth of the primitive Indian, we were not passive observers of nature, nor were we wandering bands of nomads … by and large we were active agents in shaping the land to produce prolific abundance.'[13]

The reality is that human beings have the capacity to work harmoniously with natural systems and to create greater abundance for all that lives. The belief that the Earth would be better off without human beings belittles our sacred relationship to the planet, our innate entanglement with all life on Earth. It is through an involved relationship with the land that we can begin to form a meaningful connection. We don't fall in love with people by just looking at them; the connection emerges through conversation, through the exchange of feelings, thoughts, and touch. For me, it's the same with land work. When we are working with deep respect, when we learn to listen and respond to nature, we begin to see how much we might need each other – how there are echoes of a deep and loving relationship between the human and the non-human that has been long forgotten.

Nathan Rupley is not of Indigenous heritage but is working to reconnect to the plants of his local land, to the plants of his own origins – separate from the shackles of colonialism.[14] This is crucial work for all of us, to decolonise ourselves from the inside, and reframe our view of the world through our intimate connection with the land. Decolonising has two definitions, one of which is when a colony withdraws from a state. The other is a more subtle and nuanced definition, which is to 'free (an institution, sphere of activity, etc.) from the cultural or social effects of colonisation; eliminate colonial influences or attitudes from'.[15] This is an invitation to inspect all areas of our life: our beliefs, our practices, our media, through the lens of the historically unchallenged eurocentric narrative.

Colonialism is founded on genocide of Indigenous communities, exploitation of labour, and white supremacy. It has poisoned the planet and our relationship with it. When decolonising work is applied to permaculture, it becomes about honouring nature as something we are part of rather than separate from. We do this by untangling the conditioning that has successfully torn us away from nature, by connecting with plant life from a place of gratitude and reciprocity rather than separation and power.

As Chenae Bullock, Indigenous activist and descendant of the Montauk people of Long Island says, 'our plants are in need of us to reconnect'.[16] Decolonising is a process of unlearning long held, exploitative and separatist ideas about human beings and our relationship with nature. Nathan Rupley exemplifies this in his foraging work by only taking some of what is available and reciprocating through supporting the ecosystem which allows these plants to thrive,[17] as opposed to the colonial approach to land management, where humans take more than they need with no regard for the profound peoplehood of the plants and animals around them. This work is complex and multifaceted, and will be further explored in the 'Earth Care' section, where we look at land management from a place of oneness with the natural world, which is an inherently anticolonial perspective. Through practising this continually, we may find our way back to a shared history which predates colonial control, an innate blueprint of connection to the natural systems that live within all human beings.

What we must remember is that the capitalist, colonial world we live in isn't working for anyone; we are all wounded by this system of exploitation. The ways in which we are oppressed are integral, of course. However, it is necessary to work together, to look unencumbered at our shared wounds, and to acknowledge our mutual grief and fears.

Those of us who are not of Indigenous heritage and who wish to work with permaculture have a dual duty. We must pay respect to, centre and uplift Indigenous communities as we move forward with work that was influenced by their knowledge. Beyond that, it is essential that we return ourselves to the land,[18] the specifics of which will be explored in the 'Earth Care' section of this book. It is a precarious balance to pay homage to communities harmed by colonialism, to begin to separate our identities from the colonisers, and to start to unlearn the modern and harmful view of nature as a separate entity, whilst also addressing our privilege or the violence in our histories. I think it's possible for both to coexist, though. It has to be possible, in fact, because we are standing in the face of an overwhelming force. The tidal waves of climate change have already started to drown us. We must collectivise and find ways to connect to each other and to the land now. But how do we begin this process?

For me, the process has been about relating more intimately to plants and to places. I think of Slapton Sands in Devon, a beach where we wild camp every summer. I think of the sun buzzing like a waspy halo and how we fling ourselves into the freezing Atlantic Ocean. I think of the smell of pine, the way it takes me back to the conifer forest

I grew up in, where my mum and I would cut down our Christmas tree yearly, and the pine needles would cling to her baggy cardigan. Modern industrialism has slowly and steadily separated us from the natural world, and as we lost information about plants, we lost the ability to see ourselves in them, to recognise our own cycles as we pay attention to the cycles of nature. So, we have to intentionally search for this connection wherever it manifests in our lives.

Through the slow process of identifying species with which we engage regularly, we can begin to connect intimately and lovingly with our landscape. We may start to repair the relationship between humans and nature. We owe this to the origins of permaculture, the deep Indigenous wisdom of our interconnectedness, so we must do so alongside fighting for land to be returned to those it was stolen from. There will be resources available at the end of this book to be a part of the fight for rehoming the land to its previous stewards and to hear first-hand from Indigenous voices.

In the words of Dr Lyla June Johnstone, 'I know it's not enough to simply mimic Native practices, we must also work to return some of these lands to their original caretakers. For in addition to healing the soil, we must also heal our history as a nation. And we can do that together.'[19]

If we are to view ourselves as permaculturists, we are to view ourselves as custodians of the Earth. Within that there is a responsibility to look at our past with open eyes, to look to the future we are leaving for new generations, and to remain firmly in the present, in the landscape we inhabit. We must work to be of service, to be a force of heart and healing.

To return is tricky and painful, especially when in doing so we must acknowledge a history of violence and genocide whichever side of the coin our lineage pins us to. It requires grief; it requires surrender; it requires care. But in the midst of all that is ancient knowledge which can actively stand against the systems of power killing our planet. There are seeds of resistance germinating, and we are capable of developing the skills necessary to plant them.

Invitation: Plant Identification

Forming an intimate connection with your local land through familiarising yourself with the species of plants and animals around you is the backbone of creating a thoughtful permaculture design. In doing so, you can understand how things are growing naturally, take note of the connections between them, and eventually consider how you want to get value from what you identify. And regardless of the design process, through identifying the environment around us, we are able to connect more intentionally. For example, you could learn the names of the flowers that grow in your garden, the shrubs in your allotment, or the tree you eat beneath on your lunch break.

This can be achieved through downloading free plant identification apps such as PlantNet[20] and iNaturalist.[21] Another option is to use Fields Study Council fold-out guides,[22] Collins Tree Guide, Collins Wild Flower Guide[23] and various other plant ID guides available. For identifying birdsong, there is Merlin[24] and for fungi, Picture Mushroom. Spend some time finding what works for you. You may not feel as sophisticated as Sherlock Holmes or as authentic as Masanobu Fukuoka but don't worry; I'm sure if they had Google, they would have used it too.

Chapter 3

Why Is it Important?

'Permaculture is a revolution disguised as gardening.'

– *Mike Feingold*

If you are reading these words, I'm going to assume you believe in climate change. If that's not the case, you might want to take a seat because you're in for a bit of a shock. So far, we've explored the origins of permaculture, and now it's time to look at why this practice is essential, now more than ever.

I won't spend too much time boring you with the gory details. I am in the business of hope, and whilst being informed is necessary, it can also be a dangerous game. It's all too easy to doom scroll and become wholly despondent, overwhelmed with the sense that there's nothing we can do. Sometimes that's what we need, and that's okay, but I've found it's hard to change the world whilst weeping in the foetal position.

Human-made climate change is real and it's already having a destructive impact. It was stipulated in the Paris Agreement of 2015 that global warming could not supersede a 1.5°C increase, this being the tipping point for irreversible damage.

Since then, insufficient action has been taken, and as it stands now, the planet has warmed 1.2°C above pre-industrial levels.[1] The reality of how this climate breakdown will manifest in our lifetime is mass loss of biodiversity, 99% of coral reefs destroyed, poverty, famine, and global refugee crises.[2] This isn't a far-fetched worst-case scenario for the future, it's a realistic trajectory for human beings if we continue to live far beyond our means and exploit the Earth.

What's even more demoralising is that, though the mega-wealthy and corporations are responsible for the lion's share of carbon emissions, the poorest are the most immediately affected. Whilst the Elon–Bezos–Kardashians of the world fly to space and build apocalypse bunkers, the poorest people suffer the consequences: 'The poorest 50% of the world's population contribute to 7% of global emissions, whereas the richest 1% are responsible for 15% and bear the least effects of climate change. This is climate injustice.'[3]

Unfortunately, those of us living in Western society who don't eat gold leaf cereal for breakfast and jet ski to the moon for a weekend break are still a part of the problem; the average person living in England creates more carbon emissions in one day than someone from the Democratic Republic of Congo would in a full year.[4] It is clear that wealth disparities and inequality experienced in society equate to a harsher impact from climate change, and more of this will be explored in the fair share section of this book.

So, it's all a bit scary. I give you full permission to scream into your pillow or watch bloopers from your favourite guilty pleasure sitcom, and do what you need to do to feel sane again. If engaging with these facts makes you feel guilt, fear, rage, despair, or even emptiness – that is an indication that you are a person who cares. To feel this way from a place of responsibility and will to change this reality is even more daunting – but it also makes you super sexy and cool.

'So how can permaculture save us from this hellscape, Maya?' I hear you ask. Well, small-scale, localised land management is one of the best solutions to fight ecological collapse. With permaculture we can restore soil health, build more homely habitats for species to increase biodiversity and ensure food security whilst building strong community networks. We are helping to stave off the material impacts of climate change and resourcing ourselves for the reality of what is ahead of us by cultivating the compassion and resilience required to stay strong amidst the chaos.

Permaculture promotes a necessary shift in perspective. Our desire to climb the capitalist ladder, our glorification of grind culture and our obsession with hoarding wealth are all ways of being in the world that need to be left behind to make space for a more hopeful future. Whilst corporations are far more responsible for climate change than we are, we remain accountable for our personal paradigm shifts. Permaculture is concerned with how we adapt to the crisis by returning to our local land, because climate collapse results from a globalised, fossil fuel and carbon-intensive production process. Permaculture instead asks us to be thoughtful, considerate, and minimal with what we use and how we impact the Earth, to slowly reframe our needs and desires outside of a neoliberal lens, where our value is derived from our output and consumption.

Permaculture is regenerative and sustainable, which means it does more than sustain what is already there; it helps to regenerate and rebuild what is lost. If you recycle your waste, you may feel you are sustaining resources and contributing positively to the environment. While I am not against recycling, this is maintaining what already exists within a harmful system; mass energy is expended in the recycling process, and it is not particularly beneficial for the Earth and its resources, but instead a way of greenwashing. This is defined as using marketing and imagery associated with 'sustainability', or making small changes with little to no real impact in 'an attempt to make people believe that your company is doing more to protect the environment than it really is'. [5,6] Whereas a permaculture system takes a derelict plot of land and reuses cereal boxes for mulch and plastic bottles to protect rootstock. Within a couple of years, the soils are healthy and food is available to eat. Something more subtle but equally powerful happens in this process, too. Networks are formed by sharing resources; bonds are built in conversation while digging your beds or sharing your lunch. These small moments of connection become just as valuable as the gardening itself. Permaculture enables people to feed themselves and their communities through regeneration and skill building.[7] There is something refreshingly radical about exchanging knowledge and skills and doing so within a space that feels untouchable to the hands of power. To do so in reverence for nature in its fullness is truly beautiful work.

Permaculture does not require academic knowledge or access to wealth and machinery; it transcends language and therefore can provide food security for all people in need. Permaculture is a grassroots movement, and it builds from the soil upwards. Permaculturists such as Geoff Lawton and Rosemary Morrow have taught permaculture to communities impacted harshly by climate change, regenerating deserted landscapes and resourcing communities with skills and greater food security.[8]

Morrow 'strongly focuses on non-violent methods and the design of highly nutritional gardens, easy to maintain with local resources while providing a high diversity of nutrients and vitamins to prevent diseases linked to extreme poverty conditions.'[9]

If we want to be a part of the solution, we need to look at the damage climate change has on us internally. We are living in a world of hyper-individualism, fearmongering, isolation and division. I don't know about you, but that reality doesn't exactly make me jump for joy. It's an entirely natural and intuitive response to the world we are living in to struggle with our mental health and outlook. The diagnosis of climate change anxiety is just another example of how climate change harms us. As S. Clayton states, 'focus on individual mental health should not distract attention from the societal response that is necessary to address climate change.'[10] Though our response to ecological collapse is seen as a personal problem through the lens of an individualistic world, it will only be healed through active, integrated and collective work towards climate justice.

Beyond the anxiety response to the prospect of an unstable future, there are tangible detrimental health effects felt by those currently living with the results of climate change. Climate change is causing increasingly extreme weather events and natural disasters. This is impacting individuals' mental health as well as putting them in physical danger, showing up as increased PTSD, anxiety, depression, substance abuse and domestic abuse. Effects tend to be greater for those who have experienced more significant harm, and they are helped significantly by sources of social support.[11] Common findings that weave their way through analyses of these impacts are that stress, disconnection, and the impending sense of a desolate future lead human beings to feel not very good insid e. Who'd have thunk it?

What is required to halt climate change is a complete overhaul of our current system. But alas, waiting on the powers that be to stop killing the planet feels like a relatively hopeless pursuit. I strongly advocate holding them to account, but we have to do this alongside making it healthier for ourselves in the process. I have watched many activists – people I love – wilt in the face of this often ugly and oppressive world. If the movement towards revolution erodes those who care, it's not sustainable. We have to look to build the world we dream of on the horizon and feel glimpses of its warmth on our skin to find ourselves there. This is where permaculture comes in.

In Johann Hari's revolutionary book *Lost Connections*, he shifts the lens through which we understand mental health, which has dominated our perspective on depression and anxiety for decades, from a chemical imbalance in the brain to a realistic and sensical response to a world driven by disconnection.[12] Hari says, 'What if depression is in fact, a cause of grief – for our own lives not being as they should? What if it is a form of grief for the connections we have lost yet still need?'[13]

Hari outlines nine different causes rooted in a lack of connection to what we need to function and flourish. It is important to mention that you don't have to identify with any disorders or have diagnoses for these causes to resonate; they are part of a commentary on the way the modern world is built, fundamentally failing to serve any of us. Amongst the various causes, those that apply to permaculture are disconnection from meaningful work, meaningful values, other people, the natural world, and from a hopeful or secure future.[14]

I suffer from climate change anxiety, regular old anxiety, and occasionally depression. It's not super fun and what strikes me is how normalised it is. I engage with more people who share this experience than don't. Sometimes the hollow sadness or the high-alert over-thinker feel like aliens infiltrating my body; other days, they feel like a necessary sickness trying to reveal something to me. Sometimes I feel consumed by grief for a world I want to exist in, and I yearn for a sense of belonging that seems inconceivable in our current world. Permaculture not only resists the structures that harm us environmentally, but can also work on rewilding our internal landscapes, which feel deserted. It's this place where I've built momentary havens. I've watched groups of people enter a deteriorated space and transform it into something green and extraordinary; I've witnessed emotional transformations and community support, primal screams quelled with laughter, food shared, and hungry hearts quenched.

Working towards a goal and purpose that contributes to securing our future is immensely valuable for our health. Permaculture has community as a core tenet, partially because many hands make light work but also because humans need humans. When we collectivise together in the face of shared fear whilst connecting to the wonder of nature, rare magic can happen.

In the interest of sounding as least like a cult leader as possible, permaculture is not a cure-all practice that will immediately save you and the world from impending doom. But it can offer us a lot of value when tackling the impacts of climate change, both environmentally and emotionally. It feels intuitive that we need a sense of hope through action, the ability to feel that our hands can make a difference.

Why Is it Important?

The blade that separates our mental health and well-being from the environment it exists within is forged from the same metal that severed human beings from nature. The wound will have different shapes and sizes for all of us, but it is bleeding all the same. This makes me think of an extract from one of my favourite poems, 'Sometimes a Wild God' by Tom Hirons:

> The wild god points to your side.
> You are bleeding heavily.
> You have been bleeding for a long time,
> Possibly since you were born.
> There is a bear in the wound.
>
> 'Why did you leave me to die?'
> Asks the wild god and you say:
> 'I was busy surviving.
> The shops were all closed;
> I didn't know how. I'm sorry.' [15]

When I read that, I can feel flashes of myself in the bear, the wild god, the writer, and the wound. I can see myself in the closed shop windows and the apology. A wildness is stifled in my chest, which is never liberated when howled into the stale city air. The wound doesn't heal when I attempt to salve it by buying reusable straws or signing petitions. But I notice something primal rising inside me when I put my hands in the soil, engage in meaningful conversations and connect the small act of planting onion bulbs in an allotment in Bristol to a wider web of people practising permaculture in the far reaches of the world. Through this connection to people who share my fears and take action, I am revitalised. The wild god within me is soothed. The apology transforms into a song of the potential of rain, of deserts transformed into jungles, of a heart still beating and hopeful.

Chapter 4
The Twelve Design Principles

What can nature teach us about how we want to be in the world?

In some sense, the twelve design principles are my bible, my almanack of finding solace in an overwhelming world. There is something salvaging about reading words reflecting an approach to life that actually makes sense.

Retethering ourselves to the natural world only becomes effective when we reflect on our processes and show up in our fullness, learning where we want to adapt and grow. Each design principle is explored agriculturally here, but they can apply to any area of your life. For example, are you in a relationship that feels stuck? Have you reached a crossroads in life and are not sure what the next step is for you? If you look with an open mind, these principles can offer answers that consider you in your entirety. If we accept our interdependence with all other life and attune ourselves to the sensitivities and wisdom of nature, our inner inquiry should reflect this too.

What's essential is that you value your own voice and ability to think creatively. Context is crucial because our worlds are varied, so growthful learning begins when we reflect on these insights and apply them to our outer and inner terrains. We are our own almanack, our own sacred scripture, our own guides – because we are the Earth teaching itself how to heal.

Principle 1: Observe and interact

'By taking the time to engage with nature we can design solutions that suit our particular situation.'[1]

A popular proverb is that the eyes are the window to the soul. I've always felt that about the hands, too, and I believe both, when used with intention, can be our doorways to the sentient Earth. In permaculture design, this is an essential skill to strengthen. Through an engaged and relational observation over time, we witness nature and all its intricacies and oddities. Suppose we start to notice what is happening on our land and familiarise ourselves with its inner workings. In that case, we can then recognise what adaptations ought to be made.

Without an intentional observational process, we perpetuate the systems permaculture attempts to break away from. If you have a garden space where you wish to implement a system, strut in all big-for-your-boots, and attempt to shape it directly to your will, then you're entirely missing the point. We are working with nature, not against it. Equally, if you are following a step-by-step process of implementing a system without considering the specific vegetation in your environment, then you're assuming that you can just do whatever you want and nature will obey. Observation is the key because we are first embedding ourselves in the culture we inhabit before considering where we want to make adjustments. How can you know what you must change until you've tended to what is already there? It's time to remove our proverbial boots altogether and step barefooted and open-hearted onto the soil.

This principle asks us to look at the broader view of our life with curiosity and acute attention. Observing and interacting isn't the same as passively looking. I could sit by the sea, briefly watch the waves crashing against the rocks, and be on my way. Or I could close my eyes and hear the layers of sound in the waves, the whisper that gathers into a crash and then softens into a salty sigh. I could imagine what it would feel like to be that rock kissed by the water. I could observe the rock pools and the crabs' day-to-day comings and goings, the way they creep towards the limpets and slurp them up, their bodies like sea-salt creme caramel. I could touch the rock with my hands and feel the mossy slime or the sharp edge. It goes beyond observing nature; it recognises that we are nature, and holds us in our totality as we connect with the land.

- » What can be learned and adapted through the act of paying attention?
- » What would happen if you opened your eyes to what's right there in front of you and dared to reach out and touch it?

Principle 2: Catch and store energy

'By developing systems that collect resources when they are abundant, we can use them in times of need.'[2]

When you kiss a new lover, dance under the moon or fluorescent lights, or share a tender look with a stranger. What gives you energy? What makes you come alive? We are stripped back of so much too often, shackled to our shadow. Light usually arrives in an instant, the sun beaming in a flash before disappearing behind the clouds.

- » What happens if we step outside to bask in it – despite inconvenience or poor timing?
- » What if the time to bask is always now, and when the rain is pouring down, we let ourselves get wet?

The catch and store energy principle considers where energy arrives on our land and how we keep it there. In the modern world, we rely on energy systems that exploit finite resources with little regard for their rarity. In a permaculture system, we use renewable energy sources and utilise as much energy as possible. In doing so, we can use the abundance of the past energy when we lack it in the present. This exemplifies a permanent culture: preserving what we have now to support us in the future. A belief held by some in sustainability and conservation is that human innovation will rescue us from the suffocating grasp of climate change.[3] Whilst I'm not saying that's impossible, it's equally possible that God will push the Big Red Button, or that Venus will swallow us. What I'm getting at is that 'possibility' removes us from the reality of what is happening right now. Human innovation and greed caused the environmental collapse we face, and it's very difficult to win the battle with the same blade that started the war.

Our separation from the origins of our energy renders us unable to connect the dots of our daily behaviours to their impact on the planet. If we derive value and practice gratitude for naturally available energy, such as the sun or water, we may form a direct connection with them and protect finite resources in the process. We can do this in our system by implementing water catchments, solar panels, or earthworks that guide and preserve the water.[4] What is required is a phase of energy descent rather than energy growth, where we intentionally lessen the energy we use and place the value in the wealth readily available to us on this planet, affluent in abundance as we are.[5]

Principle 3: Obtain a yield

'Ensure that you are getting truly useful rewards as part of the work that you are doing'.[6]

At the heart of the human is hunger. We are operating with the wiring of our hunter-gatherer ancestors, attuned to the subtleties surrounding us to survive. We are programmed to respond to threats, protect ourselves and feed our families. We feel hungry and want to fill our bellies in communion. These longings are often fulfilled by supermarket food, tired-eyed from our nine to fives, severed from the source of our sustenance. Our obsession with unending growth and hoarding resources is born from that primal urge. It is the same cycle, but it's distorted and disconnected. It feels intuitive, then, that if we are to build autonomous systems, a crucial element of that process is getting something out of it for ourselves. In the neoliberal view of value, yield is defined by money or power. The challenge here is to relearn yield as that which we can generate from our own soil with our own hands, to ask ourselves the question: *where do I derive value?*

Let's say you decide to plant some rosemary in your garden. In this context, the simple view of yield is being able to season your food. But what else happens throughout that journey? Maybe you ask for a cutting from a neighbour and have a friendly exchange in the process. Perhaps you sit and drink your morning coffee, watching a bee meander over to obtain its own yield. And when you harvest it, possibly the earthy perfume lingers on your fingers. Or you cook a Sunday roast, and your family gathers around the table and eats your rosemary-infused potatoes.

» What if the value of the yield isn't just in the act itself but the connection and community woven into it?

» What if you looked at all the small ways you obtain value on a daily basis?

» What if yield isn't found in monetary wealth or personal ownership, but within the heart of the animate everything?

Principle 4: Apply self-regulation and accept feedback

'We need to discourage inappropriate activity to ensure that systems can continue to function well.'[7]

When I was a child, I had a recurring nightmare. It would start with me on a boat, my mother holding me to her breast; I feel I am as tiny as a fingernail. The inky water beneath us is barely visible, yet its presence is felt. Beside me, my dad is looking upward at the moon. I am small but safe. Suddenly, we are ashore and anchoring our boat to the rocks, but before I know it I am thrown from the boat and left alone on the island. I watch my parents slowly shrink away; and I scream their names, but they don't once look back. Years later, the ache I felt on the island has stayed with me. The story of abandonment is one I am familiar with. This might seem strange to write about in a permaculture book, and you might now be wondering if I'm doing okay. Don't worry; I promise I am going somewhere with this. (But also, yes, I would appreciate some tissues and a tub of ice cream, thanks for asking.)

I have inherited generational trauma from both of my parents, shaping my story of being in the world and the relationships I build. My dad leaving means I often search for love in the dark corners of men who are not well-versed in tenderness, people I know will activate the trauma that he left behind. It's a familiar story for all of us. Even though it takes myriad shapes, we are all sculpted by our histories and what our parents passed down to us. From my mum, I also inherited resilience, the ability to find laughter in darkness, and a love for the majesty of trees. I have learned how to self-regulate, self-soothe, and give my body what it needs when that trauma arises. My generation has increased awareness of mental health and access to resources that allow us to find our way to healing. With each generation, there is a new panoply of wounds to soothe; a new opportunity to break destructive cycles. In a permaculture system, the process is similar, but with less ice cream and avoidant boyfriends.

The best example of a self-regulating ecosystem is the planet herself, who has responded to threats and challenges with creativity for millennia. She has accepted feedback and adapted to sustain her life. A permaculture system is built on the premise that if we pay attention to what the Earth tells us, we know how to respond to it deep within ourselves. We are currently receiving signals that human behaviour is damaging our planet.[8] Yet, we continue to hunger for what is beyond the remit of our resources and are seemingly unable to connect this to the inevitability of ecological collapse. The proverb 'the sins of the fathers are visited unto the children of the seventh generation' anchors this principle in the duty of stewardship and the acknowledgment that negative feedback takes time to emerge, so we must pay acute attention.[9] We are living through the tumultuous repercussions of relying on finite fossil fuels. If we responded to that feedback and applied it to ourselves, we could regulate our usage of finite energy or install solar panels and utilise energy from the wind. We are burdened with the mistakes of a consumerist culture which has eroded our soils, poisoned our waters and exploited our labour. If we self-regulate in response to this, we can minimise our unethical consumption and tend to our soil. This principle asks us to self-regulate in response to the signals of distress we are receiving, from a place of self-awareness and responsibility.

- No Juniper Tree has ever known ego, so humility is written into its DNA. All it knows is: grow. All it knows is: be. What if we were like Juniper? So willing to adapt to remain alive?
- How do we regulate ourselves and accept feedback?
- What if the journey of our own healing is inseparable from the healing of the Earth itself?

Principle 5: Use and value renewable resources

'Make the best use of nature's abundance to reduce our consumptive behaviour and dependence on non-renewable resources.'[10]

In the city, beneath these concrete boxes, there is an underworld ululating. Life is brewing in the soil and forcing its way through the cracks. This growth is unfamiliar to many because it doesn't ask anything of us in return. For so long, we've been told a story of love which is transactional, co-dependent, expressed largely through lavish outpourings of material matter. We view value as something to own and constrain love to the parameters of possession. We prune bushes in our front garden and resent the bramble for its persistence in spilling out its edges.

I've never seen anything more beautiful than life happening for life's sake. This is what this principle speaks to. It invites us to rekindle our love for nature by being mindful of what we use and *valuing nature for what it is beyond our usage.* Like the kiss of the sun, the shade of the tree, or the possibility of the snowdrops which land like love letters, spreading news of the gathering spring. The proverb 'let nature take its course' is a core creed of this principle.[11] The image used by the Permaculture Association to illustrate this principle depicts a horse which could aid the soil fertility and transport resources around your site, yet the more subtle and poignant value derived here is the love shared between the human and the horse. It's about an empathetic relationship forged between living beings, unconstrained by yield or output.[12]

» What renews you?

» What if we consider relationships to be symbiotic as well as transactional?

» What happens when we view our love for the Earth as unconditional?

Principle 6: Produce no waste

'By valuing and making use of all the resources that are available to us, nothing goes to waste.'[13]

How do we define waste in a world so enamoured with the cutting edge? We buy upgrades for our functioning phones and throw our old ones 'away' as if 'away' is some far-off bin in the sky untouched by human hands, and not a landfill crammed with toxic waste. We are not well acquainted with the reality of where our waste goes. We gobble up everything in front of us like an unstoppable Augustus Gloop, but we will face a much more severe fate than Dahl's hungry German boy if we don't get our shit together. We have to look at our waste right in its blood-red face and not look away.

Bill Mollison defines waste as 'an output of any system component that is not being used productively by any other component of the system'.[14] This is a lesson in mindfulness and self-awareness as much as it is minimising waste. We must confront ourselves with the reality of what remarkable life is already ours and where we can better utilise our 'waste' products so they add value to our system. Consider the humble earthworm and how he feasts on waste that supports the fertility of the soil, and our system becomes more prolific with life. Waste management is a crucial facet of whole-systems thinking because we consider the cyclical management of the inputs and outputs in our design system.

- What could you make better use of in your life that you'd usually neglect or abandon?
- Is there anything you assumed was a 'waste' product that can in fact add value?

Principle 7: Design from patterns to details

'By stepping back, we can observe patterns in nature and society. These can form the backbone of our designs, with the details filled in as we go.'[15]

My mum befriends the spiders in the corners of her cobbled cottage. I've always admired that about her because I am terrified of spiders; there's something alien about them. The ones that creep me out the most are daddy long legs, not made better by the fact that their name makes them sound like lanky porn stars. Despite my fear, spiders are brilliant beings, and when they're not plotting their evil schemes, they construct intricate webs of silk. Each is unique in its craftsmanship but conjures a ubiquitous image of spokes and spirals. If we are to imagine a spider's web, we are likely picturing something similar, but the specifics will be different.[16]

With this lens, we consider our whole system simultaneously with the details within that system. If we do this when we reflect on ourselves and the culture we exist in, we can make pertinent adaptations by holding first our mutuality and then our singularity; we can hold a broader understanding and notice how this filters into nuanced relationships. We can observe the whole picture through the initial stepping back and then consider the details. In a permaculture system, this is essential because by looking at the fuller picture, we can understand the relationships between our decisions. If we are writing the story, we must consider all of the scenery – the characters and their origin stories. If we do so thoughtfully, paying homage to the human and the blackthorn, we could rewrite a new narrative into being. We could be the authors of the story of our salvation.

» How does stepping back and considering the whole inform how you make decisions?

Principle 8: Integrate rather than segregate

'By putting the right things in the right place, relationships develop between them, and they support each other.'[17]

If you were to walk out of your front door right now with a ball of string and plot the connections between each living thing you saw, you'd soon run out of string and probably be very tangled up and confused and resent me for suggesting such a ridiculous activity. However, there is value in materialising the invisible connections that bind life together. The connections between all animate beings are essential to the functioning of the system, they are as integral as the beings themselves, yet they are often unseen or unacknowledged. Applying this principle to our design becomes a practice of actively fostering fruitful, co-supportive relationships between the living entities within the system. Permaculture is a whole system outlook that contradicts modern science's tendency to isolates singular components to study.[18]

We tend to believe the story of survival of the fittest, which pits living beings against each other in needless competition with no actual winners. This story glorifies human beings' ability to overpower other living beings and champions one species of strength, disregarding our reliance on the web of life. It is a cultural story so pervasive that it seeps into the narrative of how we define ourselves. We celebrate competitive relationships over collaborative ones. We praise defining features that separate us from each other: you're special if you do something no one else can do and can only do it by bettering others.

» What if we celebrated our ability to cooperate?

» What if instead of placing winning on a pedestal, we valued our ability to communicate, reach a compromise and care for each other?

'The whole is more than the sum of its parts' is a simple message, but it dramatically shifted my perspective. It indicates the value of symbiotic relationships and how they add more value than possible without them. I think of the wolf and the raven and how they support each other to feast on prey. The wolf helps the raven by checking out the scene and piercing open the prey's flesh. The raven aids the wolf by keeping an eye from the sky, alerting them to danger.[19] Without the support of each other, they would be far more vulnerable and hungry. This indicates that cooperating can be an evolutionary advantage. It is the same story for people; we are inherently social beings and would not exist without our networks of connection. We must celebrate our ability to be in alliances with each other rather than in competition.

Principle 9: Use slow and small solutions

'Small and slow systems are easier to maintain than big ones, making better use of local resources, and produce more sustainable outcomes.'[20]

I'm a sucker for a quick fix, and I find myself quickly bored if an endeavour isn't immediately gratifying. I don't blame myself for this because it's a product of the world I exist in. Culture moves at a rapid rate; I often feel like I need to run ragged just to keep up, tripping over my shoelaces in the process. But the Earth is unconcerned with fleeting fads and fast-paced feats. She is in the pursuit of homeostasis, of slow and steady winning the race. In the lifespan of our planet, we are as fleeting as the flicker of an eyelid, as fragile as an eyelash. I picture the human race in its modern manifestation as a hamster on a wheel, running ever faster and faster, burning our energy and resources and quickly running out of steam, but getting nowhere.

- What if we just stepped off the hamster wheel?
- What happens if we stop running and stand still?

It's difficult to give ourselves over to the moment we are in. In doing so, we relinquish control, and the fear that we might lose track of our purpose or to-do list creeps in. But therein lies the beauty of stepping off and slowing down; the path we are on takes a different shape. It becomes sloppy with mud, violets and brambleberries seep in from the borders. At the end of the way, a face resembles yours, but wolves are in their eyes, and their smile is a silver half-moon. They are smiling and beckoning you forward.

» Who do you see at the end of your path?

Our view of the system we create becomes something completely different when we value slow, incremental solutions over big-business-hyper-speed fixes. We can embody the patience and steadfast power of our planet. We do so by valuing local produce where we can because slowing down also invites us to zoom in, gather at our local forest or farm shop, and keep ourselves as close to the origins of our resources as possible.[21] If we expect the system we create to provide immediate results, we will likely feel frustrated and give up. The use of fertilisers exemplifies this. We may use fertilisers to harvest a good crop one year, but it contributes to soil nutritional depletion for years to come. When we use manure and create compost full of minerals, we slowly build a foundation of ever-growing resilience and abundance. The short-term yield should not supersede the long-term reward of slow and thoughtful implementation.[22]

We have a lot to learn from our elders: the trees, the ancient soil, and the big big sky. When we humble ourselves and welcome patience and curiosity, we can build a system attuned to the planet's timeframe.

» What if there was something radical in our rest?
» What if the world kept on spinning, but our heads didn't?

Principle 10: Use and value diversity

'Diversity reduces vulnerability to a variety of threats and takes advantage of the unique nature of the environment in which it resides.'[23]

It has become increasingly apparent that monocultures are fragile and highly vulnerable to threat.[24] This tells us something: to stand alone without support weakens us. To stand alone endangers us. The use of polycultures and the encouragement of biodiversity in a permaculture system places value on the unique adaptations and evolutions of all the living entities which make up the system.[25]

> 'The spine bill and the hummingbird both have long beaks and the capacity to hover – perfect for sipping nectar from long, narrow flowers. This remarkable co-evolutionary adaptation symbolises the specialisation of form and function in nature.'[26]
>
> – *David Holmgren*

We can say the same for people. Our unique adaptations as individuals can benefit and enrich our relationships. Cultural difference plays a role here too. For example, my Italian housemate Valentina can be direct and fiery, qualities I admire about her. But they have, in the past, struck a dissonant chord with the uptight British woman in me. Through this relationship, I have found more confidence and ability to state my needs, and Valentina has learned to practise more acceptance and compromise. From this perspective, our differences influence each other and result from the cultures we are born from.

Celebrating diversity creates a more vibrant world of tenacity, passion, connection, music of every shade, and feeling in every layer. Diversity opens the world, and its odd innards spill out of its centre. Diversity not only enlivens the world we exist in, but it also strengthens it. When considering a whole system, one deficiency might be supported by another's ability. When we respect the unique origins and evolutions of each living being with which we share our land, we see the world for what it is: a strange and beautiful alchemy of difference and survival.

» What happens when we celebrate diversity in our inner and outer worlds?

Principle 11: Use edges and value the marginal

'The interface between things is where the most interesting events take place. These are often the most valuable, diverse and productive elements in the system.'[27]

What blooms from the borders is often misunderstood. Consider the recent commodification of queer culture and how that which was once on the margins has been gradually placed in the global centre. I am indebted hugely to queer art. Any artist, regardless of their identity, is too. So much of our cultural language is shaped by artists who have been marginalised, subjugated and gate kept from cultural spaces. We have seen this, also, with Black artists throughout history. Often, unique art born in the quiet corners of our world eventually gets appropriated and repackaged to appease whiteness and our dominant capitalist narrative.[28]

There she goes, banging on about capitalism again! Well, get used to it, friends. We have a responsibility to draw connections and parallels between our threats. The same force that polices queer, black and brown bodies is the same force exploiting workforces, corrupting the planet and depleting nature. Pay attention to the radical joy born in opposition to this force. The sheer resilience, fierceness, and adaptability of these communities is awe-inspiring. And it tells us something crucial about how we should be in the world.

We must value the marginal and centre the life that grows in those small spaces without rebranding it or reshaping it to our will. So much fascinating activity happens on the edges, and this is true of ecological communities too. More life and vibrancy often occurs when two ecosystems collide. This is called an 'ecotone'. Picture the places where the land meets the sea; tidal estuaries are born, and within them are cultures of algae, niche plant growth, and unique and diverse minerals that feed the whole system.[29] When we ignore the potential of the edges, we miss the opportunity to learn the complete picture of our system and use the space available to us. If we value the edges and the marginal, we learn they are as valuable and rich with life as the centre, if not more so.

» What is happening on the peripherals of your vision?

» How has your life specifically been shaped by the marginal?

» When you investigate your own edges – places within yourself which are unseen or untended to – is something blooming within them that could benefit you?

Principle 12: Creatively use and respond to change

'We can have a positive impact on inevitable change by carefully observing and then intervening at the right time.'[30]

» What if we let ourselves be a little clumsy? What if change wasn't an impending threat but an intriguing inevitability? What if we saw ourselves as the caterpillar and the butterfly, always at the end and the beginning of a journey?

As we consider implementing an intelligent and holistic design system, we must consider how we respond to change. We must look to the Earth and its adaptations, at how change is entwined into everything. Any sense of control we garner from viewing ourselves as fixtures is illusory. We are impermanent, malleable Earth bodies, and nothing on this planet of ours is stable or guaranteed.[31] It's time we accepted that fact, scary and sweat-inducing as it may be. By accepting that change is inevitable, we can use it to inform how we adapt. Instead of feeling at the mercy of change, we listen to what it is telling us and learn how to respond creatively and sustainably in ways which benefit the entire ecosystem.

We must view this reality with a bit of lightheartedness and play. We are learning how to work with our planet's splendour, doing crazy things like asking the trees questions and building systems that work against the mainstream approach. So lean into the absurdity, acknowledge this planet for what it is: savage, wonderful and in a constant state of flux. When we do this, we can view mistakes as opportunities to sink deeper into our collective ecology.

Invitation: Drawing & Journalling on the Design Principles

This activity is adapted from one created by Sarah Pugh, one of the founders of the Shift Bristol course. Sarah was an institution of urban permaculture and an emblem of the tenaciousness and humour that carries us through this work. She was a caring mother, a wise and thoughtful leader and an absolute hoot. Whenever I feel disillusioned with my inability to make more expansive waves in this world, I think of Sarah. The way she responded to life's difficulties with grace and hilarity taught me that it's possible to do a whole lot with one little life. Since Sarah passed on from a rare brain tumour, I like to imagine her atoms gathered at a mountaintop, somewhere expansive and overseeing, so she can continue her life's work of facilitating beauty and rising above it all.

For each of the design principles, there are images attached. This is so the principles can be recognisable beyond language barriers and implant the meaning of each principle more firmly in our heads.

For each principle, draw out your own symbol you feel embodies that principle. It helps to stick these in a place with which you regularly engage, like your journal or bedroom wall.

Journal on each principle by responding to these prompts:

» What does this principle mean regarding land management?

» How does this principle relate to human beings and society?

» What does this principle mean to me personally?

[illegible]

[illegible] impact [illegible]

[illegible] different [illegible]

[illegible] each [illegible] principle [illegible]

[illegible] or [illegible]

[illegible] design principles [illegible]

What [illegible]

[illegible] about [illegible]

[illegible]

EARTH CARE

Chapter 5
The Design Process

'Though the problems of the world are increasingly complex, the solutions remain embarrassingly simple.'

– *Bill Mollison*

When I arrived at Gasworks Studio on the first day of the Shift Bristol course, I was freshly twenty, nervy as hell, and wearing an impractically floaty skirt, dressing to materialise the butterflies in my stomach. Shift Bristol holds two courses, one shorter Permaculture Design Course and the longer Practical Sustainability Course.[1] I was about to embark on the latter. Everyone gathered together in a lumbering circle, cradling cups of tea. The room had a sense of apprehension, a flurry of new voices and nerves. The space itself is beautiful. It can be found behind an unassuming door of a cul-de-sac in the inner city. Behind it lies a haven, a temporary pause, a wooden floor speckled with multi-coloured cushions, bric-a-brac mugs and windows that filter in dusty light. Out the back, there is a large garden. The surrounding neighbours knocked down their walls so they would have more green space to gather, plant and connect. I feel warm when I picture the garden walls crashing down. I want to curl up in that feeling like a cat.

I remember being scared that I'd be kicked out for not being 'sustainable enough', or something. I am partial to Coca-Cola and sometimes wear clothes from Primark. I wasn't exactly the poster child for being environmentally conscious, even though I cared very much. I didn't even know what a trowel was. I remember it distinctly because I laughed out loud as I thought it was a funny word. There are two things you can glean from this. Firstly, I don't have a very sophisticated sense of humour. Secondly, if I can learn the permaculture design process, then anyone can.

The formal design process is intentional and intuitive, focusing on sustained observation and considerate implementation. It does not require pre-existing knowledge or an extensive understanding of gardening. The strategies outlined throughout this process are intended to be simplistic and accessible. This chapter leads you through a dual process. First, you will create a base map that lays out what you already have available. The second stage concerns what you want to do with your land, which will be built upon your initial map. The following chapters will explore the elements you will implement in this design, such as soil, water and plants. You may want to understand these in more depth before returning to this chapter to add them to your design.

To develop as a permaculture designer, you must constantly reflect on the learnings and apply them to your context, so how you engage with this process is up to you. The invitation is to develop whole-systems-thinking because that is the essence of permaculture design, in which each living being relies upon and supports the other. We are anchoring ourselves in the ethos of locality, renewability, and the perspective of a permanent culture – whereby the systems we build benefit the entire ecosystem beyond a momentary advantage. We are developing ourselves as holistic gardeners by learning practical, compassionate and integrated skills which can withstand the toxic tide of intensive agriculture.

The most active way to learn the design process will be through ongoing connection to your land and a Permaculture Design Course, information on which will be provided at the end of this book.

Creating a base map

To create your base map, you will need paper, a ruler and coloured pens. You also need tracing paper for the overlays, which will be explored later. First, we want to create a scale drawing of your site, which provides a layout of the shape and size you are working with and each component you place on the map. Remember that you do not have to get this to an exact science; we aren't architects or mathematicians.

Firstly, you will need to measure your site. You can use a tape measure or pacing, depending on how specific you'd like to be. Pacing is using the length of your natural stride to calculate your measurement. You take a step and measure the length of that step, and then you can multiply that by how many steps you've taken.

Scale drawings translate the size of your land onto the page. The scale you use depends on the land you are working with. An A4 piece of paper should be sufficient for a base map. For small gardens, a scale of 1:20 will work. For medium-sized spaces, 1:50. For larger areas, potentially 1:100 will be the most useful to you. In any case, choosing easily divisible numbers will make the process far more straightforward. For example, if your garden is 8 X 6m and you use a 1:50 scale, you will end up 160mm X 120mm – which could fit on your page. If you find numbers baffling like me, you can use scale converters online, which will do the calculations for you.

Once you have an outline of the space on your page, you can add the following elements from this checklist. Not everything on this list will necessarily apply to you.

Base map checklist[2]

- Boundaries: internal (e.g. fence through property), external (e.g. where does your property end?).

- Buildings access: external (e.g. gate into the site) and internal (e.g. a path throughout the site).
- Plants: broad scale and small scale – only note what you will keep.
- Water: broad scale (e.g ponds and streams) and small scale (e.g. where is there a water tap?).
- Landform: Degree of slope and aspect. This will be more relevant if you're working on a larger scale. There may be existing contour/ terrain maps available for your site. An easy way to do this is by going on Google Maps and clicking the terrain layer.[3]
- Coordinates: To chart the movement of energy, it's helpful to add the coordinates of North, East, South and West to your map. Ensure that the North is at the top of the page to orient yourself. The offering here is to get a little creative. Different colours will help plant the map in your head and clarify each component. Hopefully, it'll be a little fun too. Try not to worry about it looking perfect. It's nature; it's supposed to be scruffy and outside of the lines.

Sector overlays

These will be added to your tracing paper layer.

Note where energy flows through your system: sun, water and wind. Each is a sector and would be on a separate overlay paper. For example, the sun sector[4] shows where the sun moves throughout your land. This helps you to be site-specific and attuned to natural cycles. You can notice where the shade will be or where you want to plant vegetation. You're looking to **catch and store energy**;[5] noting where it arrives in your system and how to make the best of it whilst it's there or deter it where it's not useful.[6]

Zones

Zoning is a way of designing your site concerning how much maintenance or energy it requires. For example, if you are planting herbs you intend to use often or a vegetable bed that requires regular watering – essentially anything with high input or usage – you place them as close to 'zone 0' as possible. Your energy is valuable and should remain at the forefront of your design because building a system around an unrealistic version of your capabilities is impractical. And also because you are trying to boost nature's well-being alongside your own. As always, don't make it more difficult for yourself than necessary! Zoning is a way of considering your capacity as instrumental to the maintenance of the system.[7]

Zones 1–5 measured by levels of use

This is the Permaculture Association's list of zones:

- Zone 0: Centre of activities – the house. This is high maintenance, high use and requires a considerable investment of time and energy.
- Zone 1: Annual plants, herbs, compost, plant propagation, construction and maintenance, bike shed, other high-use activities, greenhouse. Regularly watered.

- Zone 2: Dense planting, poultry and small livestock, orchard, polytunnels.
- Zone 3: Large water storage, main crops, sheep, cows, and field shelters.
- Zone 4: Forestry, wood pasture, dams, forage.
- Zone 5: Wild zone, where nature is in charge and where you go to learn and harvest only that which is abundant.[8]

Here is a Base Map of my garden including a sun sector overlay and zones

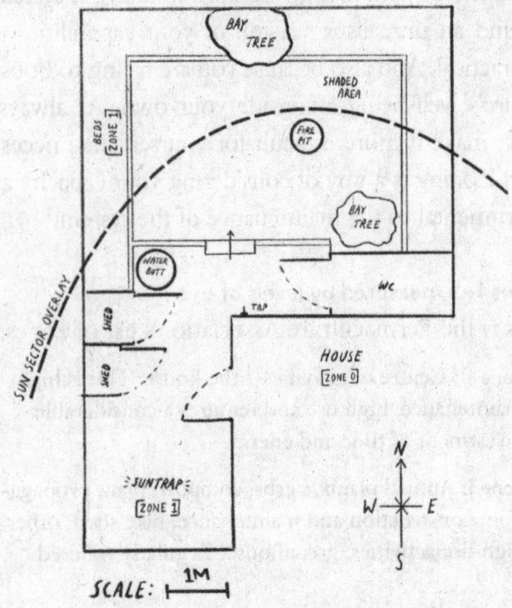

Invitation: Sensory Mindfulness

Your senses are windows. Beyond each of them, there is an open sky waiting. Your hands are the architects of touch, revealing a world unsullied by words, tangible with textures and tenderness. Your eyes bring you colour, the beauty of its brimming bouquets. They witness the fleeting blue of the kingfisher as it glimmers on the lake; a whole animated sphere of awe awaits. Your nose is a storyteller and time traveller. The honeysuckle, dressed in buttery yellow, seduces you into sweetness. You smell the tang of seaweed and salt, and suddenly you're at sea; the scent of a lover brings you to your knees. Taste is an offering which connects us to our means of survival. Your warm, wet mouth is a primal provocateur, urgent for deep kissing and a fusion of flavours. Sound brings you music, the whisper of waves, the dialect of birdsong and the cadence of each unique voice.

Many advise at this stage of permaculture design that you spend an entire year **observing and interacting** with your land.[9] This provides the space to connect with your landscape intimately, note where the sun travels, or where you feel moved to sit and eat your lunch in the shade. What spaces are easy to access and used regularly? This is an opportunity to build a strong relationship with your land, unfettered by forward thought, enacting the principle of **using and valuing renewable resources**.

It may not be possible for you to wait a whole year. In a world so fast-paced, it makes sense if you want to hurry into action. Maybe your space is small, and you don't feel it is necessary. You are your own designer, so go with what is appropriate for you. But remember that time is your companion and not a threat. You don't need to outrun it. When you pause and befriend the time you have available, you're more likely to make thoughtful decisions. Consider the principle **use slow and small solutions**.

The invitation here is to intimately connect to your landscape through your senses. Step out into your space. Maybe it's a local park, back garden, acreage, or wild woods. And walk. Nothing high-tech or complicated, just one foot in front of the other (If that is not possible for you, this invitation can work just as well whilst sitting down). As you do this, begin to zoom in on each sense one-by-one and, where you can, separate them. Walk with your eyes first: notice the colours, the layers of patterns and textures. Then sound: what can you hear nearby? Your feet on the ground, maybe a twig breaking? Beyond that, are there distant sounds? Slowly move your attention to each sense individually before arriving at a stop. Find somewhere to sit that feels comfortable and, if possible, private. You are in the company of your senses and the natural world and for now, that's more than enough. Once you are seated, give yourself over to all of your senses at once. Bask in their offerings as they interact with each other.

If you return to this practice regularly, you can start to attune yourself to what is happening on your site. You can pay attention to where the sun and the water flow, which bird species gather there, or where there is high wind and sun traps. This information shapes your connection to the land and how you wish to work it.

Site survey

This is another phase of the process that considers what might be available to you that isn't necessarily needed on the map but provides a more comprehensive analysis of what your site has to offer.[10] Remember the principles **use and value diversity** and **make use of edges and value the marginal.**

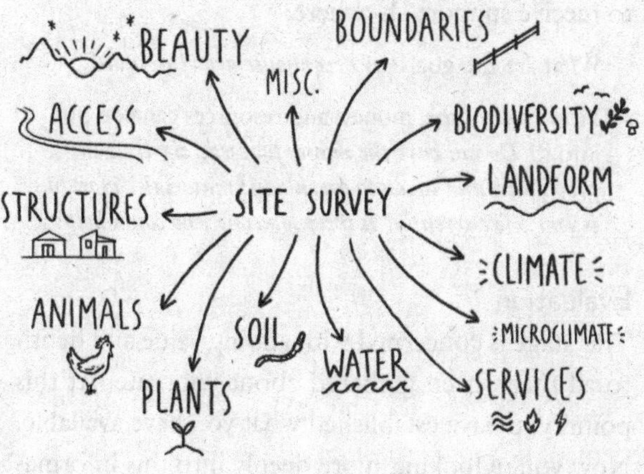

Ruby Scott-Geddes, adapted from *Earth Care Manual* (endnote 11)

Questionnaire

At this stage, you need to ask yourself what you currently have available to aid in design implementation.[12] It's important to centre your capacity throughout this process. So often, when we think about our available resources, we consider external objects instead of our arcane inner worlds. You may have all of the saplings for the orchard, but if you're burnt out, you won't have the capacity to bear fruit. Our emotional states are as temperamental as the weather but, also like the weather, they are integral considerations and assets in your design process. I invite you to also consider your relationships as resources. Where you lack something, is it possible to receive support elsewhere?

» What are the goals? *A greenhouse growing salad.*

» How much time, money, and resources can you put into it? *Do you have the money for seeds, the time to propagate, and access to greenhouse materials? How busy is your life currently? Is there someone who could help?*

Evaluation

This stage is concerned with adding value and depth to all that's been gathered about your site. At this point, you have established what you have available. Now you're looking more deeply into this information to apply it to your design.[13]

SWOT analysis: strengths, weaknesses, opportunities, threats[14]

This analysis is a thorough pros and cons list. Strengths and weaknesses look at the internal pros and cons of your situation, essentially what is within the remit of your control and within your immediate access. Opportunities and threats are external factors which you may not usually consider, and looking at these can broaden your perspective on your decision. Say you want to have chickens in your garden. Strengths could be obtaining eggs and improving soil fertility. A weakness could be a time constraint or lack of space. Opportunities could be a want for local eggs in your area. A threat could be foxes wanting to eat your chickens. This analysis allows you to look inwardly and outwardly at your circumstances to form a holistic analysis.

Needs analysis[15,16]

This analysis considers what is going into and coming out of your system. It's a way of assessing the value of different elements and whether they can be cyclical – can the outputs feed the inputs? How can you utilise the outputs in ways you hadn't previously considered? This can be used for any element in your system and help you to decide whether it will be useful or wasteful, which will likely be an ongoing inquiry encouraging us to consider the

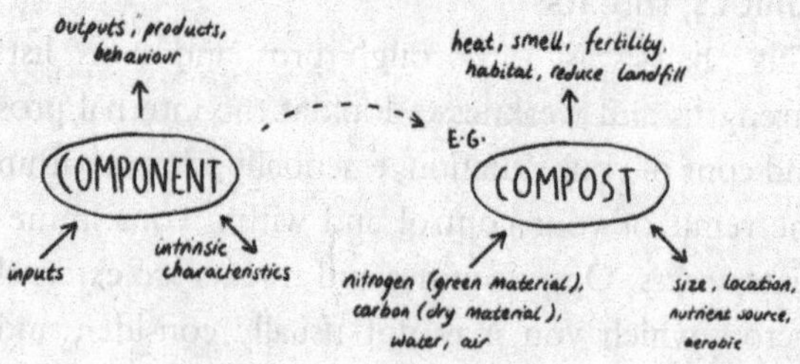

design principles **produce no waste** and **integrate rather than segregate.**[15]

We've been in the world of graphs and logistics for some time now, so I'd like to remind you to look outside for a minute. Take a deep breath, take stock. Unclench your jaw, roll your shoulders. In the next phase, you finalise your design. This may be too early for you, and you may want to tread a little further with me before you know what you'd like to implement.

If you're ready, I invite you to root yourself in this moment. So rarely are we awake whilst on the precipice, so often blind to which crossroad moment led us down a particular path. The process of design is intricate, messy, perplexing and rewarding. You begin to form the land, and new colours and shapes arrive. You may even transform your dreams into something tangible. This is tricky alchemy, but so worth the trouble. Some of the fog and the foliage may be clearing for you, the path revealing itself. Breathe in the air before you step onto it.

Design proposals

After the evaluation, it's time to think precisely about what you want to implement and how to get there. This is where you consider your needs and how you intend to **obtain the yield** that you want. It's a process of stepping into a future vision and then taking incremental steps back to see how you can get there, which is to **design from patterns to details**. Below is an example of how to formulate this process.

Aims – *what do you want?*
For example, self-sufficiency, firewood, beauty, biodiversity.

Concepts – *how will you meet that aim?*
For example, coppicing wood, using only native species.

Details – *What are the specifics of this?*
For example, exact boundaries of the area that you're going to plant, the species you would like to welcome, habitats that would invite them in.[16]

It's time to get your pens out again. Looking at your base map, with the information gained from the analysis, you have a document which lays out your space. Now it's time to design what you want this space to look like. This is where you plot what you want to plant, where it will go, and where new structures will be built. This will be illustrated on another overlay.

Re-evaluation

This will come after you have implemented your design and considered what's working and what isn't. It's important to remember that we're never really finished.[17] It's like never-ending homework. Aren't you glad you picked up this book? The principles to keep in mind here are **apply self-regulation and accept feedback** and **creatively use and respond to change.**[18]

If it seems that not much is working, remember that you haven't failed, my friends; you have tried, which makes you something special. Pay attention to what feedback nature offers and how to understand it better. At every stage, we're learning languages of listening and attuning ourselves deeper and wider. Look at you go! You adaptable, imperfect collection of cells in an abundant and scary world! Look at you trying to make growth happen, even in the face of a challenge! I'd give you a big old snog if that weren't wildly inappropriate and literally impossible.

Chapter 6
Soil

'If a healthy soil is full of death, it is also full of life.'[1]

– Wendell Berry

I want to tell you a story about finding love in extraordinary places. To write a book on nature is to write a book of unlikely friendships. To form a loving connection with nature in a world which only tells the story of human love, and primarily *romantic* human love, can feel unfathomable. I want to tell you a story about how I became devoted to the soil, but more than that, I want the story to sound reasonable to those who read it.

The story starts with the loss of my beloved childhood dog Nova. Like the cosmic phenomenon of his namesake, he was a flash of radiant energy. Nova had one blue eye and one brown, white hair with blobs of auburn, and a tail like a whip. When you stroked him, he'd make a seal-like noise and malt hair all over you. He was full of love and so wonderfully strange. This nonhuman connection, I suppose, was the prequel to this book. It taught me how love could be overflowing and bountiful and ask nothing of you except that you love it back and, of course, fill its bowl with dinner. For this small act of service, I got unwavering companionship in return. I found something refreshing in a connection founded on such willing and intuitive reciprocity. This opened up a tenderness in me beyond the complex, cerebral nature of human relationships.

When I was a young adult, Nova passed away in his sleep, and we returned to Haldon Hill, the community where I grew up, to bury him. This is where I spent my girlhood; I had my first period, made my first friends, agonised over unattainable love interests, and became infatuated with Beyoncé. Just off the motorway, you could find caravans and buses rebuilt to be permanent homes, outdoor sofas, firepits, mini flower gardens, and children running barefooted amongst the grass and gravel. There was also a lot of Special Brew, theft, drug abuse, and a looming shadow often found in communities of outliers and addicts. I am writing of its beauty here, but to do so without speaking to the darkness would be a disservice. I've had far too many infuriating conversations with middle-class hippies who idealise my childhood and paint it in rosy hues. My upbringing was outside the constraints of capitalism; it instilled a potent connection to nature and formed me into a headstrong, heart-strong adult. But it certainly wasn't all white-linen-clad peacemakers playing tambourines and yodelling. There was light and dark here – hippies and heroin addicts, trauma and healing.

Foxgloves speckled the hedgerows, and tadpoles squirmed in the troughs of water that lined the roadside. Beyond the vehicles and the colonising rhododendrons, wooden steps led me down to the pines. Hidden amongst them was an abandoned well, long unused. Licked with lichen and moss, it stood like a concrete imposter that had slowly befriended the forest and transformed into something green and wild. I remember walking Nova down there to find bluebells blanketing the forest floor. I like to think he also found them beautiful. But beyond that, I like to think the bluebells, in their own way, knew their beauty. This was where Nova made his first memories, so it felt fitting he was taken there to rest.

I cried myself to sleep for weeks when we lost him. It was the first loss of my life, and I couldn't reconcile that what was once his animated body was now still. But slowly, a shift happened. I would walk to a hillside in the village where I then lived. At this hill's top is a crumbling oak, with mossy knuckled branches and a sense of true grandeur, half decaying into the earth. I meditated on this tree for a long time; half dead, half alive, half of the soil, half of the sky. The oak felt liminal yet tangible, in some place mythical and in-between, beyond the black-and-white binaries of life and death.

I had never found much salvation in religion that took the concept of God and placed it in the hands of the clouds. When I lost Nova, my Grandad, and then Dan, it became apparent that God wasn't in the sky but in the soil. Or rather, God *is* the soil. This was the turning point of the story. I became utterly intoxicated with the mud beneath my feet. I zoomed in on the earthworm's gummy bodies as they writhed. I noticed the different consistencies of mud: grey sludge, chocolate brownie, and lightning cracked.

It may sound odd, but I feel a genuine kinship with the soil. A tenderness once reserved for the loved ones I have lost now comes back to me when my hands and feet are on the earth. I feel that familiar reciprocity beyond language that I felt with Nova. If I nurture the soil, the soil nurtures me. I wonder how the world would differ if we saw our love as limitless, beyond the boundaries of human connection. It might be the salve for loneliness or the doorway to belonging. Within a single handful of soil, there are more microorganisms than all the human beings on Earth.[2] How unbelievable is that? There is a hidden constellation of relationships at work, right beneath our feet.

When I want to hear Dan's laugh or Nova's howling, I take myself to the woods. I examine the silver birch, its paper moon skin flaking. I picture celestial bodies floating through the soil, their veins bleeding silver blood and birthing the mycelial web from which all grows. I imagine heaven as a fresh apple, a punnet of sweet strawberries, a bouquet of parsley. I make a fruit salad of my grief, eating it with my feet on the earth, the clouds leaning in for a bite. The leaves on the trees go on falling. Somewhere not far off, a beloved utters their final goodbye. And I am all of it, the fruitful fragility of life, the cycle of loss and renewal. The soil holds this ultimate paradox because decay allows life to grow, and it is with this awareness that we tend to the soil in our garden. We know that we are a part of the cycle because when we grow life, we also grow eventual loss. We must recognise that we are in service to that which sustains us, and without caring for the soil properly, we will not obtain sustainable or valuable yield.

When we facilitate growth systems, we do so with climate change resilience in mind. Soil health is one of the most important elements of your design system because no life will be left to grow without healthy soil. Soil is a non-renewable resource: it stores far more carbon than the atmosphere, regulates the Earth's ecosystem, builds flood resilience by absorbing water and provides 95% of our food.[3] Intensive industrial agriculture has led to approximately 60% of organic carbon depletion in arable soil.[4] Threats to soil health are compaction, erosion and nutrient loss.[5] When we consider this reality through the lens of permaculture, we tend to the soil with a sense of responsibility and view these threats as opportunities for growth and renewal.

Soil types

There are three distinct types of soil: clay, silt and sand. The ideal garden soil would be a loam of these three: 20% clay, 40% silt and 40% sand.[6] If that is the case for you, here's your gold star! Now please stop showing off and get to planting your carrots. You'll unlikely have a dream loam, however, so you will have to figure out your soil type. From this, you can learn what is ideal for planting and how to improve the health of your soil.

Mason jar soil test

As is the way with permaculture, we don't need high-tech devices to do our calculations. All you'll need is your soil, a spade, and a clean mason jar with a tight lid. It depends on how extensively you would like to conduct this test. You can do a singular test if you have one area soil or one for each bed.[7] If you have a larger space, it might make sense to do a few different tests to obtain an overall measure of the soil you're working with.

You want to dig about one spade's depth. Half-fill the jar with soil from this depth and fill the rest with water, almost to the top. Ensure the lid is tight and shake it for several minutes to keep all particles suspended.[8] Set your jar aside for several hours, preferably overnight, so the particles can settle. They will separate into layers of clay, silt and sand.[9]

Reading your results

The bottom layer will be the heavier particles, sand, and rocks. The next layer will be the silt particles. Above that are the clay particles and organic matter floating on the water's surface.

Using this diagram, calculate your loam type[10]

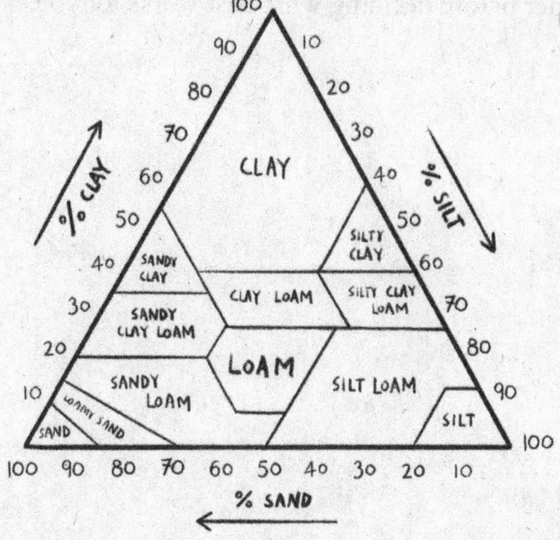

Your calculations:

20% clay, 40% Silt, 40% sand = Dream Loam[11]

30% clay, 60% silt, 10% sand = Silty Clay Loam[12]

15% clay, 20% silt, 65% sand = Sandy Loam[13]

15% clay, 65% silt, 20% sand = Silty Loam[14]

Composting

Regardless of the soil type, you need to get composting as soon as possible. The best way to improve soil health will be to feed it yummy nutrients. To create healthy and productive soil, you need a good balance of carbon (brown materials) and nitrogen (green materials).[15] The degree to which you compost will depend on the scale of your system. In the chart on the opposite page are some factors to consider before deciding what best works for you.

Compost type	Outline	Pros	Cons
Hot compost	A big compost pile with the correct balance of green (nitrogen) and brown (carbon). Turn the compost approximately once a week to aerate it and keep it hot. The desired moisture is that of a wrung-out sponge: damp to squeeze but not leaking water.[16]	1. Breaks down quickly due to the heat. You can have functioning compost within two months.[17] 2. The heat kills weeds. For example, you can put in nettles that have already gone to seed, which won't affect the compost.	1. Requires a large amount of space. 2. Hot compost is at least one cubic metre in size, so this might not be possible for your site.[18]
Cold compost	Pile you throw on every day. Again, the correct balance of carbon and nitrogen.	1. Very low input: you don't need to turn it. Just leave it to do its thing.[19] 2. Makes great use of daily waste: You can throw yow your kitchen scraps on and cardboard recycling onto the pile. 3. Cold compost takes up less space than hot and can be whatever size you want.	1. Takes a lot more time to create compost.[20]

Worms

My beloved wriggly friends! An alternative option is the use of a wormery to create your compost. You feed the worms your leftovers, and they do the breaking down process. This is ideal for urban settings because it can easily fit into a small or crowded environment. It is low input because you add kitchen scraps, and the worm castings create nutrient-rich compost.[21]

Mulching

Mulching is essentially anything that you put on top of your soil. As always, with permaculture design, we observe how nature works and how to mirror this in our system. In nature, there is no bare soil;[22] life in its bountiful forms will bloom into any space fervently. We can learn a lot here about how to take up space and use available soil optimally.[23]

Here are different types of mulch and how they might be used in your system:

Clearance mulch

A clearance mulch is used to clear a new area of weeds so you can start planting. Considering that you likely want to be ready to plant in spring, beginning your clearance mulch around autumn is ideal, but it can be done anytime. The intention is to cover the soil area in something which suppresses plant growth. Consider what resources you have that will be low-cost and environmentally considerate. For example, you could use a leftover tarp or black plastic sourced second-hand, anything that blocks the light from the plants. This way, you don't have to exhaust yourself by pulling out weeds.[24] Remember to utilise local resources.

Grow-through mulch

A grow-through mulch suppresses weeds but allows you to grow something alongside it, which also improves soil health. It's a triple whammy, my friends! A good way to create a grow-through mulch is 'lasagne mulching'. This is a process of layering your green and brown material. Using cardboard is ideal here as you're separating what you're planting from what you're trying to suppress. You plant directly into your green material and you may need to cut a little hole in the cardboard to assist growth. Be mindful of what to plant in a grow-through mulch. For example, you wouldn't want to add root vegetables as they take up a lot of space, and it will work more effectively if you're suppressing less pervasive weeds such as grass.[25]

Maintenance mulch

A maintenance mulch is ongoing in an established growing area. It's a way of protecting the soil alongside what is already growing. The benefits of this shielding are numerous: it can regulate water levels, suppress weeds, and provide insulation for the soil when it's cold, as well as build up and break down organic matter, which benefits the soil structure.[26] An example of a maintenance mulch is placing straw around your lettuce.

Green manures

Green manures are something that you plant to enrich the soil, particularly if it's too compact or lacking in nutrients. You can plant green manures in your crop rotation (see the 'plants' section for more information). You grow them for one growing season, and when they are on the cusp of flowering, you chop them down with the roots in the ground, leaving the plant to break down in the soil. At this stage, the green manure is abundant in nutrients which will make the soil super happy and say things like 'yum' and 'that's delicious'. Well, that's what I imagine, anyway.

Examples of green manures you can plant

Long term: alfalfa, perennial ryegrass, lucerne, sainfoin, red clover, white clover.

Winter: common vetch or tares, trefoil, grazing rye, mustard, phacelia, field beans, buckwheat, ryegrass, and tares.

Summer: fenugreek, mustard, lupins, vetch, buckwheat, crimson clover, sweet clover, Persian clover.[27]

No-dig gardening

No-dig gardening (or no-till gardening) is often a staple in soil management within a permaculture system. That's because it requires minimal energy input and allows nature to do the work it's been perfecting for millennia. In a no-dig system, the application of compost is your version of mulching. The benefit of no-dig gardening is that you're not interfering with the elements aiding soil health. The microbiome, mycelium, worms and bugs can get to work without being bothered.[28]

Another benefit of no-dig gardening is the suppression of weeds. When tilling, you often break up and spread weeds, so they multiply and must be picked frequently. With no dig, adding mulch will suppress light for weeds, which means less work for you. There may be a need to till in certain circumstances; for example, if you have compacted clay soil, digging at the beginning is sometimes necessary as it loosens and aerates the soil. Or, if you have sizable organic matter such as rocks, they must be moved before you can plant anything. No dig gardening does have restricting factors, as creating a lot of compost costs money and requires a larger space.

However, this approach imitates nature and focuses strongly on the health of the soil and the value of your energy and time, so I advocate for this. If you want further guidance, look into Charles Dowding, renowned for his prolific no-dig garden.

Invitation: Soil Visualisation

Take off your shoes and socks and plant your feet on the earth. You can stand up or sit down, whatever feels comfortable. I invite you to close your eyes or lower your gaze and consider the web of life beneath you. Start by focusing your attention on your feet, move your toes and notice the texture of the ground beneath you. Continue to deepen your visualisation and move through the layers beneath you with your imagination. As you move through the first layer of topsoil, you may see the cord of weeds, rock fragments or organic matter decomposing. Consider how the mycelium moves, how the worm wriggles. Spend some time deepening your breath, and sink further into the visualisation with each exhalation.

» What can be learned from focusing your attention on the earth beneath you?

» Do you feel connected to something beyond yourself?

Chapter 7
Water

When I am in the water, I am wordless. 'Less' implies a lack, something to be desired. It's more like a necessary absence or a fulfilling blankness. When I am absent of words, I am in the company of the uncultivated and the untethered. Water is a shape-shifter. It can fill you up, wash you away, hold you close. Just now, sweaty and stressed as I leant over my keyboard writing this, I heard the rain beating against my window. I took myself out to my back garden and sobbed in the downpour. I was held and washed away at once. What compelled me to run outdoors half-naked, I'm not fully sure. It could have been my attempt to mimic Kate Winslet's desperate romanticism as she ran through the wet hills of Dartmoor in a mud-stained light blue gown; love lost tends to bring out the dramatic in us. Such monumental, unquenchable sadness feels worthy of the weeping sky. But I think something more subtle, some elemental stirring, led me to it. It was the same urge that flings me into the freezing ocean in the winter; the same urge that leads me to bathe in the mornings, when I am heavy with the sorrows of the world.

I like to sit when the tub is barely full and shiver a little, slowly warming up as the water rises. I notice that the curves of my body are easier to look at through this lens. The dimples of my cellulite become adornments of the water. Something like the imprints the ocean leaves on the sand. Something like the way you can feel someone on your tongue seconds after they pull away— a beauty defined by its impermanence. As I salt the bath water with tears, I am as unconstrained as the wild woman in the sea. Soon the day will bludgeon me. Soon I'll resent my dark circles as I pass car windows on the street. I'll feel grief-ridden, undesirable, impossible to love. But not when I am with the water; for a fleeting instance I am glorious. It strikes me that regardless of the form in which it arrives, water quenches the deepest of human thirsts – to become undone and unbounded, to be fluent in a language of wordlessness.

There is something magnificent about water, how it swallows sorrow, the way it remains unconcerned with its size. It changes with no resistance and flows in an ever-connecting, ever-changing form. Water is a place where I am as insignificant as a pebble – humbled by the transience of my human pain. I doubt the water cares much for my agony, and that is precisely what brings me to the edge of the sea, knelt in a clumsy prayer, asking questions I don't want the answers to.

Water

Water is one of those attributes, like health when we have it, that we take for granted. We watch the rain fall in swashes and let it wash away our topsoil without catching it and using it somewhere useful. In the West, we flush our excrement out in freshwater. At the same time, vast amounts of people do not have access to safe drinking water in places such as Ethiopia and Papua New Guinea.[1] That disparity is jarring, and it illustrates how deeply wrong our approach to nature's precious resources is. Only 14% of rivers in England are deemed to be of a good ecological standard, and the vast majority are teeming with raw sewage.[2] When you boil this down it's horrifying: we shit in freshwater and swim in raw shit. Apologies for that image, but this reality should encourage us to preserve and respect our access to clean water.

When using water in our permaculture system, we are looking at how to make the most of what we have while we have it. Water is a cyclical resource, constantly evaporating and falling from the sky in the rain. We interact with a tiny percentage of the water cycle, only able to use approximately 0.003%.[3]

Water available to you

» *Surface flow* arrives in your system through the rain. It's the most renewable and sustainable access to water you have, so using it in your system is preferable.[4]

» *Groundwater*: This is underground water and what you're tapping into if you have a well, for example. This is a finite resource that can take centuries to renew itself. This water is far less sustainable, so you must be thoughtful about your usage.[5]

How to catch and store your water

Put simply, the motto is: 'slow it, spread it, sink it'.[6] This means slowing the water down as it enters your system, spreading it around your site so it's being used to its fullest potential, and sinking it into the soil.

The first thing to consider is your relationship to water and how you use it. Our culture is mindlessly wasteful, and this is no single person's fault; it is crucial that we instead consider our place within the bigger picture. To perpetually widen our gaze can easily numb us into inaction, completely disregarding our ability to change, but this broader view is useful in informing our adaptations. How can we use what is already there, or what is usually seen as a waste product of our systems? For example, would it be possible to have a compost toilet instead of using freshwater toilets? In doing so, you could gain nutrition for your soil and utilise a seemingly wasteful product without further wasting water.[7] Another simple strategy is the catchment of rainwater. Could you use stored rainwater instead of a freshwater hose to water your garden or wash your dishes? Or could you use wastewater, also known as 'grey water',[8] such as washing-up water, bath water or laundry water? As long as you're using eco products, water which would otherwise have gone to waste can be used to help support life in your system. Remember that for vegetables, you will want to filter this first, but it's fine to be used on trees.[9]

Invitation: Journalling Activity

Think of the rain trickling down, how it holds so much capacity for life, how it has the power to wash away and make way for new cycles. Water allows itself to be held, and so much can prosper from this place. What does the water teach us about our own lives?

Here are some reflective questions to consider:

» What do you want to catch and store?

» What do you want to let go of?

Beyond this reflection, I invite you to jump into a body of water. Or when it's next raining, step outside into it. Or even set your shower to cold for a few seconds, anything which switches up your usual engagement with water. In doing so, you may practise gratitude, open your eyes to something new where you have not looked before, and bask in the torrent of nature, as it goes on flowing.

Earthworks are adaptations you can make to your land to store and direct the water flow so that you are losing less and using more.[10] It is likely that earthworks will be more useful in bigger spaces, but regardless of the size of your site, they illustrate a crucial consideration of water in your system. One symptom of climate breakdown is increased extreme weather events, including flooding and drought.[11] We ought to build systems which account for these changes. Preserving water and directing its flow is a way of ensuring stronger climate resilience within your design.

A typical example of earthworks is the implementation of swales. These are small sunken channels, similar to ditches, that are 'designed to intercept moving surface water and allow it to infiltrate into the ground'[12] and are used when you have some sort of gradient.[13] On your base map, you may have noted your contours, which will help you here; the process of implementing swales entails digging a little ditch on the contours or slightly off them. This has the effect of catching the water flowing downwards and spreading it across the land, which has many benefits. Swales are particularly important if you have a steep slope on your site, because heavy rainfall in one area will erode the soil[14] and wash away nutrients if not appropriately mitigated. Swales can instead build durability to water damage;

you can plant amongst the swales, which promotes higher value from the space with little additional effort as the plants are immediately watered. Using this method, you can plant trees, shrubs and generally hardier vegetation and leave them mostly unattended.[15]

» Here is an example of what planting amongst swales looks like:[16]

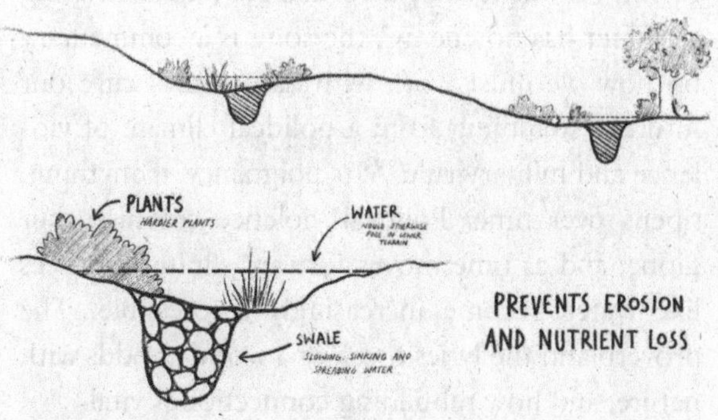

Water features can encourage biodiversity. In addition to bringing the blossoming beauty of birdsong to your doorstep, this strengthens your system and welcomes in greater abundance. Building a pond is a simple way of creating a home for wildlife.[16] Water features are also a reminder of stillness: they invite birds and bugs and quiet thoughts. Introducing what we find beautiful, bringing us back to our bodies and the body of the earth, is essential in a design system. In doing this, we enrich our lives and deepen our connection to nature and her precious elements.

At the heart of our work with water, we must remember to respect it. The Nigerian musician and activist Fela Kuti, the forefather of the musical genre Afrobeat,[17] spoke of the battle between humans and nature in his song 'Water No Get Enemy'. Influenced by a Yoruba Proverb translating as 'water has no enemy', the song is a commentary on how we must work with nature to secure our future,[18] stemming from a political climate of violence and military rule.[19] Its poignancy, if anything, ripens over time. Political violence colonises our globe, and as time moves forward, finite resources like water become increasingly inaccessible. The proverb and the lyrics speak of a world at odds with nature, and how rebuilding connection is vital.

If water had a voice, it would talk in a gravelly whisper, a cadence of ease that comes only with the expansive perspective of time. It would remind us of our ability to hold space and let go, of our innate flexibility and capacity for colossal change.

Chapter 8

Plants

Sunflowers are expert optimists. When I look at them, I feel lighter, more able to digest the bitterness of the world. There is a science to this. Plants are champions at growing towards the light. In science speak, this is called 'phototropism'. To me, it's 'embracing hope' or 'not giving up'. The sunflower is the attention seeker, loud in its cheerfulness. But all plants seek light in different ways; it's in the DNA of all flora to survive, even the peace lily with its pearl white flowers, which thrives in low light conditions. Maybe the hope isn't merely in a flowering, the yellowing climax. Perhaps it lives in the seed, the stork, and the subtle inner work. Maybe hope is inseparable from survival. Maybe, within the roots of all of us, there is an ancestral impulse that lends itself to light.

Invitation: What does your Photosynthesis look like?

This activity allows you to write about the different elements of your life that support your growth. Journal on any of these prompts that call to you.

» **Sunlight**: what are the sources of light in your life? Are there people or practices, TV shows or songs that make you smile? When you think of 'feeling sunny' what comes to mind?

» **Carbon Dioxide**: what keeps you breathing? Are there any fundamental elements of your life without which you'd find it difficult to cope? This is an opportunity to write about them and celebrate them.

» **Water**: what feeds and nourishes you? Does anything give you a sense of purpose? What fills up your cup? When you feel like you're running on empty, what do you do to emotionally hydrate yourself?

» **Soil**: what grounds you? What makes you feel safe and held?

Through this reflection, I have learned how much is required for me to flourish. My strength and hope grow through an interplay of countless factors; I am an unlikely accumulation of co-support. As living beings, we are interaction incarnate – interconnected individuals, inextricable from each other yet uniquely our own. Like the sunflower, each petal is distinctive, yet the same universal forces of light, water, and soil nourish each one. The sunflowers are great gurus in flaunting; they invite you to shine bright, to show off. But I've never seen two beside each other and compared their shades of yellow, judging which stood taller or grew higher. I hope we can view ourselves in the way of the sunflower, see the work that contributes to their growth, and how their flowering is no less impressive because they were supported along the way. Plant life is the plumage of light, the flourishing pinnacle of interwoven work, and the flower is made more beautiful when it belongs to a meadow.

The idea of an individual working their hands until their bones are brittle, or the success story of a lone wolf battling against all odds to come out on top, are familiar tropes in our collective narrative – and ones we revere. These stories translate to land management, too. The use of monocultures in industrial agriculture is indicative of a cultural script of singularity. It's a maddening tale and also deeply sad. In reality, a wolf may go through periods of solitude in his life but spends most of his existence with the pack.[1] And when he roams, he still belongs to his community. To step alone onto the track, find the power of your voice, and stand on your own two feet are valuable elements of the human experience and phases we may enter into willingly. But we ought to do this with intention, knowing there is a family to which we belong. This tells a different story to the enforced grinding of colonial land control, a story in which we are weaker if we need each other, in which we must nourish our own deficiencies and heal our own wounds.

Permaculture advocates for polycultures and thoughtful planting so that all the flora you place in your system support each other.[2] Polycultures are built on the premise of symbiosis; different plant niches will help one another to flourish. This highlights each plant's value, celebrating differences and their ability to benefit everyone in the system. In this way, nothing is lacking, there is room for all to grow, and no one has to break their back to make it happen.

Companion planting

Companionship is a fundamental need for all life. Companion planting promotes health in your system by diversifying nutrients, contributing to higher yield, deterring pests, making practical use of space, and encouraging biodiversity.[3] An example of companion planting is the Three Sisters: corn, squash and bean. This planting strategy was developed by Native Americans and illustrates the intrinsic ethos of co-support within Indigenous land work.[4] The Three Sisters have different attributes, needs and tastes, yet they lovingly support each other to grow through sharing their space and resources.[5] Each is uniquely beautiful, each uniquely supportive and supported.

The beans need to be of the pole bean variety, the corn should be a sturdy species such as sweetcorn or maize corn, and the squash should be vining squash instead of bush squash.[6] You plant them by creating a mound of soil, placing the corn in the centre, with the beans circling it, and the squash planted at the base of the mound.[7] The corn creates a structure for the bean to climb, the squash shades the soil and deters weeds and pests, and the beans fertilise the soil with nitrogen. You, too, are a sibling in this family and therefore also support the sisters to grow together more harmoniously.

Other examples of companion planting are alliums besides root crops to deter flies; cucumbers with nightshades to prevent weed interference; and lavender alongside tomatoes to promote pollination, to name a few. I like to picture the tomato excited to encounter the lavender, knowing she will bring bees and a sleepy seductive scent. I imagine the alliums standing firm and the flies fearing their military musk. I picture the squash, corn and bean gossiping in whispered tones about the potatoes in the bed beside them. Companion planting is a source of growth, support and safety. As you tend to these plants, you tend to relationships, watering the seeds of connection and building a supportive family.

Perennials and annuals

> 'Be yourself. Especially do not feign affection. Neither be cynical about love; for in the face of all aridity and disenchantment, it is as perennial as the grass.'[8]

These lines belong to the poem 'Desiderata' by Max Ehrmann, written in 1927. The poem explores themes that, like the grass, are timeless. He writes of love as perennial, which is to say a staple – something that sustains you. All artists are on their quests to define the ineffability of love; it's a game we play that we know will never really end. The lines in this poem, though, come closer to defining it than I would ever dare to. Because what could love possibly be if not green and enduring? What if when we planted perennials, we were planting seeds of love? There is no greater love than to feed and be fed, to know the familiar face of reciprocity, the fruiting bodies of loyalty, returning time after time to endow you with blessings.

Perennials are your long-term partners, your ride-or-die in a permaculture system. They require little input, are instrumental for healthy soil and often have higher nutritional value than annual plants.[9] They are the elders of your system and have grown uninterrupted for long periods, so they embody the experiential strength one only garners from longevity.[10] They fill the 'hunger gap' often found in early spring; when there is a lack of abundance, perennials keep you fed.[11]

The principal reason for having annuals in your system is that they offer many delectable treats you might like to eat.[12] If perennials are your loyal partners, annuals are your sexy side pieces. I think if a permaculture system self-identified, it would be polyamorous. The tomato would let you go and have your summer fling with the basil or the sunflower, knowing the home grows stronger through various connections and that you'll find your way back to them to endure the cold together. Obviously, that's easy for the tomato to say because I assume it's never been cheated on or worried that it's not as sexy and mysterious as the basil leaf.

Pest control

In designing permaculture systems, we are unlearning internalised stories that pit us against nature. Once you start to view the world through this lens, it's shocking how deeply these narratives of separation are embedded within us. We are supposedly lords of the system with our enormous brains and egos, fighting off all competition for our crops. This mentality filters down to everything, even the smallest critters.

When managing pests in your system, consider that sharing a little with them is okay. If the slugs want to nibble on some of your leaves, and you still have enough leaves for yourself, why not? A famous Bill Mollison quote is 'You don't have a slug problem. You have a duck deficiency!'[13] This means that if you mimic the wider ecosystem of nature and thoughtfully consider what you plant and where you plant it, the system takes care of itself. This is far easier and more sustainable than harmful pesticides, which kill off your pests but also damage crucial creatures like bees.[14]

Familiarising yourself with your pests lets you know when they are a threat and when your plants require protection.[15] Not only are you staving off the risk in doing so, but you are also deepening your awareness of the richness of life around you. If I didn't have the cabbage white butterfly laying eggs on my cauliflowers, I wouldn't have looked into their life cycle and learned that the male butterflies court the females by flaunting their flying skills, doing a seductive dance in a zigzag formation.[16] I also learned that, unlike other butterflies, they are a risk to vegetables when in their larva stage.[17] These considerations allow you to connect more intimately with the life in your system and learn where adaptations are required. In this case, using netting or companion planting with strongly scented herbs like coriander and fennel are forms of pest control.[18]

Another pest control option is 'catch crops', often more viable in larger spaces.[19] This is a process of planting something specifically because the pests find it really yummy and great, so they feast on it and you don't have to worry about them munching on your food. For example, you could plant marigolds approximately seven metres from your tomatoes and cucumbers; the scent of the flowers will draw in the nematodes, who would otherwise nibble on the roots of the vegetables.

Crop rotation

A crop rotation is a way of maintaining annuals in your system whilst keeping the soil healthy by preventing the depletion of nutrients.[20] This process has a plethora of benefits: it can work as a pest control, improve soil health, reduce maintenance and support in obtaining yield.[21] It involves rotating your annual crops through different beds, providing each area with the nutrients they need (particularly nitrogen[22]), staving off pests that establish themselves in your soil over the winter,[23] and preventing disease build up in your beds.[24] Essentially, it's a way of keeping pests and diseases on their proverbial toes, a bit of a creepy image, I'll admit.

Plant families in a crop rotation

- **Solanaceae**: *potatoes, peppers, tomatoes, aubergines*: they are most likely to develop issues with fungal disease within the soil e.g. blight.
- **Brassicaceae** (cabbage family): *cabbage, cauliflower, broccoli, kale*: they are hungry plants which will deplete nutrients when grown in one spot for too long.
- **Alliums** (onion family): *onions, garlic, leeks etc*: like root crops – carrots, beetroot – alliums are less resilient to disease if grown in the same spot.
- **Legumes**: *peas, beans*: are also essential as they fix nitrogen into the soil which will benefit all of the plants within the rotation.
- **Green manures**: *see soil chapter.*

Whether or not you choose to implement a crop rotation, they remind us that if we carefully inquire about each plant we implement, we build a more robust and beneficial system. We are preventing future risks of disease and pests by building stability into the system from the offset, rather than enforcing whatever we want without forethought and then tirelessly battling against the ramifications of such carelessness, which is a pretty good description of intensive agriculture.

Here is an example of how you could establish your crop rotation over a three-year period. As always, you will be your own guide throughout this. You know which vegetables you want, you know your soil types and the scope of your environment. If you incorporate the different families I have offered here and consider their functions, you can adapt this system to fit your needs.

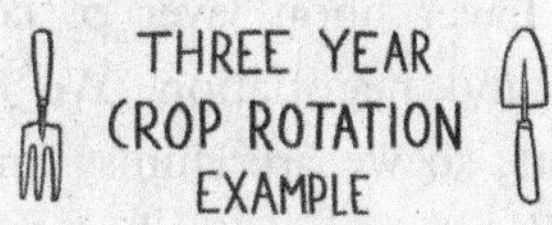

BED/AREA	YEAR ONE	YEAR TWO	YEAR THREE
A	POTATOES	LEGUMES, ROOTS + ONIONS	GREEN MANURES
B	LEGUMES, ROOTS + ONIONS	GREEN MANURES	CABBAGE FAMILY
C	GREEN MANURES	CABBAGE FAMILY	POTATOES
D	CABBAGE FAMILY	POTATOES	LEGUMES, ROOTS + ONIONS

Forest gardening

Forest gardening is a schema designed to mimic the ecosystem of a forest whilst including as many edible plants as possible.[25] The implementation of a forest garden is dependent on scale, and it might not be viable for you, but like the forest herself, this approach has a lot to teach us.

As you walk through the forest, canopies of leaves speckle light onto the decaying log where the woodlouse roams, and dark green vegetation houses the nightingale whose sweet song echoes through the layers of brown, green and yellow. And there you stand amongst it, nutritious soil underfoot, engulfed in the gifts of all the senses, a two-legged observer in a spectacular sphere of homeostasis. Layer upon layer of conversation, collaboration and negotiation. We are aspiring permaculturists, so we are clumsy imitators of a wise world. We are trying our best to learn from the teachings of nature, and reciprocate the abundance by building sanctuaries for her many gifts to find a home.

So, what is the forest teaching us? How to create a regulated, healthy system, promote biodiversity and use and share space consciously.[26] When creating a forest garden, we think creatively about using our space for greater abundance and diversity. We may do this through stacking or trellising, using tall and small plants alongside each other and utilising vertical spaces.[27] We may also embody these lessons by taking ourselves down to the woodland and observing how the space is occupied, and what entangled layers are at work if we look a little closer. Layering is the most crucial lesson amongst the many unknowable wisdoms of the forest.

Here are the most common seven plant layers with examples provided for those in temperate climates:[28]

The seven layers

- Upper Canopy *(Sweet Chestnut)*
- Lower Canopy or Sub-Canopy *(Crab Apple)*
- Vines and Climbers *(Grape)*
- Shrubs, and understory bushes *(Blackcurrant)*
- Herbaceous perennials and annuals *(Mint)*
- Ground Cover *(Strawberries)*
- Roots and Rhizosphere *(Ground Nut)*[29]

Plant guilds

Looking at plant guilds is a way to be specific with what we need and how we can meet that need. A plant guild refers to a particular niche or service a plant provides.[30] At this stage, our design is becoming more specific and tailored to our requirements.

- **The nitrogen fixing guild** has symbiotic relationships with bacteria on their roots, so can convert atmospheric nitrogen and make it available in the soil.[31]
- **The accumulator guild** mines the soil for nutrients through a deep tap root, which will add said accumulated nutrients into your soil when put into your compost e.g. comfrey for potassium, phosphorus and nitrogen. Other examples include nettles, dock, sorrel or mustard.[32]

- **The biomass guild** provides carbon quickly! For example, woody materials.[33]
- **Shelter guild**: Can overlap with biomass guild, used for blocking, repelling, reinforcing, protecting, erosion control e.g. windbreak / swales.[34]
- **Repellant guild or attractant guild**: can repel pests and welcome beneficial insects.

> 'We ourselves are part of a guild of species that lie within and without our bodies.'
>
> – *Bill Mollison*

Alongside promoting the health of plants, there is scope to improve our health by rethinking our internal systems, where we place value and where we are supported. Alongside considering plant guilds, I invite you to apply this process to yourself: what do *you* need?

- What are your guilds?
- Where do you need protection?
- Where do you yearn to be nourished?
- What is available to you, internally or externally, that could help you meet that need?

Plant growth is indivisible from our own. Plants photosynthesise and clean the air for us to breathe, and their ripened bodies feed us. They are healers;

the roots of all medicines live within them. They are full of colour and aromas that sweeten our lives. They inspire the poets and house the songbirds. They blanket and intoxicate us; some can even transport us to psychedelic underworlds.[35] Without plants, I would not have the hands to type these sentences, nor the appetite for wildness which compels me to write them. I grapple with this quest constantly, how to define the undefinable majesty of the green world? How to articulate my adoration for the hyacinths and the rosehip flowers – those blossoms which work their way into the chamber of my heart? I have not come close to answering this question, and why would I want to? Answering questions is the duty of the logical, and something far more expansive lives at the heart of this endeavour. I'll take myself to the woods, run my hands along the riddles of the bark, and attempt to decipher the song of the thrush as she rushes past; roll my eyes at my brain and its relentless musings and laugh in the company of the leaves.

Chapter 9
Animals

I was terrified of chickens as a child. In the mornings, as I walked to get the taxi to school, a man called Ron, who was as close to a redneck as it's possible to get when you're English and can't catch a tan, would let his chickens out of their coop. They were ex cock-fighting chickens, so they had a chequered past and didn't play by the usual rules. They would peck at my legs whilst making that jarring warble from their bulbous throats, moving in a tormenting slow bob which unsettled me to my core.

When I was at a homestay in Nepal, nestled at the foot of the Himalayas, I would tend to goats and chickens in the mornings. We would wake early when the day was at its coldest and eat chapati in complete quiet. The only sound came from hands as they moved from bread to mouth. I noticed other tales emerged when I wasn't nervously filling space with my words. My hosts' – Pramilla and Shanti's – hands told a story more intricate and evolved than mine. They had the softness of a mother's hands as they methodically rolled dough, and the hardship of a mother's hands, weathered from years of soil tending and sacrifice.

On those quiet mornings, the mountains were all mist. Not the light mist I knew from home. This mist had gravitas. It arrived like a slab of smoky marble, cloaking the day in an unmoving blankness. I would pass the cob toilet with the corrugated iron roof, the corn husks and shrubs, the sliders strewn on doorsteps, the tattered prayer flags swaying on clothing lines, and find my way to the goats and chickens. There, I would feed carrot leaves to the goats, and watch as they munched joyfully. I would stroke them, and we'd exchange quiet pleasantries: I'd ask them about their family and where they came from, and they wouldn't respond. A refreshing break from the endless small talk one endures when backpacking.

My next job was to clear out the chicken hut, add some straw and food scraps, and collect any eggs that had been laid. As I entered the coop for the first time, I was wary, literally walking on eggshells as they crunched beneath my feet. I was on a quest to step out of my comfort zone when I travelled, to try new things and take risks. For a normal person, that might look like spontaneous motorbike road trips or bungee jumping. To me, it was kneeling down on a pile of straw and picking up a chicken.

Initially, my clucking friend flapped frantically, but when I stroked him, he quickly relaxed. My own fear also dissipated almost instantaneously when I actually paid attention to him. Have you ever examined chickens? I realised that they are warm, simple, and utterly silly creatures. The bobbing of the head transformed from menacing to loveable. It was official; I was enchanted.

The closed-loop relationship of feeding the chickens leftovers and eating their eggs for breakfast distinctly differs from how we commonly consume food. Animals are exploited, abused, mistreated and then slaughtered. We are very removed from these origins of the animal products that we eat. It is cruel and also environmentally harmful; the production of meat accounts for nearly 60% of greenhouse gas emissions from food production.[1]

Indigenous approaches to land management, the blueprints for permaculture practice, weave honour and reverence into every aspect of land work.[2] Native Americans speak of the 'honourable harvest'[3], which is to ask permission and recognise the weight of taking a life to sustain one's own, acknowledging that it is indeed a burden and not something to be taken lightly. Understanding this responsibility looks like caring for the ecosystem these living beings inhabit. Through caring for them, they care for you.[4]

We do not stare down the barrel of the gun or hold the bow and arrow in our hands. We do not bow our heads, express our gratitude, and use every morsel of the deer to feed our families and keep ourselves warm. We buy meat pre-packaged from supermarket aisles in a place of complete disconnection from its origins and utter disregard for its value. Therefore, I respect individuals who choose to show up for the environmental movement by not eating animal products. It reduces carbon emissions and doesn't perpetuate a harmful and unethical food system.[5] Veganism or a plant-based diet is one way to step more lightly on this Earth and not buy into systems of harm.[6]

Food is deeply personal and specific to individuals, informed by many things, from dietary restrictions and financial circumstances to cultural influence.[7] It can easily be a divisive conversation firmly tethered to our identity.

While camping on an occupied road in the financial district at the Extinction Rebellion protests in London, I was working alongside a conflict mediator. There was an instance where two different camps were engaging in conflict: the vegans and the farmers. Both came from completely different viewpoints of how an individual should be environmentally and ethically conscious, yet were bound by the same fight. Once they could reach a place of solidarity over their struggles, they saw through the spitting rage of conflict to the soft waves of connection. We are all human beings, we all care, and we are all here because we don't know what else to do.

I try to embody this lesson as I move forward with my activism and care for the planet. The way you view the management of animals in your system is entirely your choice. I believe that having animals in a permaculture system has many benefits. It is a lesson in untangling the human you are from the society you exist within. Humans have orchestrated a deeply harmful food industry which is exploitative and cruel, but individual human beings themselves are not these systems.[8]

Animals benefit non-arable land by quickly adding fertility, so we must consider alternatives to obtain this without them.[9] Whilst our current land management approach uses expanses of land for livestock where it could be better utilised for healthier and more diverse vegetation, both can coexist in a permaculture system.[10] You can have cows and goats amongst your grass and shrubbery. We can untether ourselves from an unethical food system by modelling relationships with animals that are respectful, reciprocal, and beneficial for all living beings within the system.[11]

Invitation: Meditative Fox Walking

Animal trackers move through the forest silently to observe the wildlife around them.[12] Treading softly through the woods can rekindle a connection to the animal inside us, the primitive longing to feel a part of the ecosystem rather than an intruder.

'In the modern world, we move all wrong' writes Erik Assodurian.[13] The point of fox walking isn't to theatrically mimic the fox, but to walk in a meditative way, focussing intently on the movement of the feet so as not to startle wildlife.[14] If you can, doing this barefoot will allow you to tread more softly and connect you to the oracle of the earth underfoot. I advise doing this in a place of soil and wilderness: the woods, your back garden or a local park.

This is a meditative practice, so interpret this in whichever way works for you. For some people, attempting to rid the mind of words can be anxiety-inducing. For some, it's a prayer to a higher power, or simply something to scoff at. All are welcome here. The process of fox walking has many stages to it; you have to take it slow and pay attention, so the act itself invites you gently into the present moment.[15]

» **'Bend your knees'**[16]: this absorbs impact, strengthens the leg and allows you to move incognito.

» **'Take short steps'**[17]: because you are shoeless, taking short steps allows you to move more consciously, and consider whether it's safe to take a step forward. Small steps allow you to retract easily if necessary.

» **'Walk with your feet pointed forward'**[18]: this helps to maintain a balance.

» **'Walk in a straight line'**[19] with your feet astride this invisible line at all times. They will be shaped by the landscape you are walking in, but keeping this in mind can help maintain balance.

» **It's time to take a full step** once you have all these elements in check. You start by gently placing the foot's outer edge down and moving inwardly to the ball of your foot. Once this feels safe you implant the heel and find yourself full-footed on the floor. This ensures your step will be painless and won't arouse noise.

» **Repeat this process** until the wild woods enrapture you, or your feet are too cold to carry on.

How to select the right animals for your site

On a minimal holding where your main output is vegetables, the question might not be which animals to keep, but whether to keep animals at all. If you are already sourcing manure externally, and not from somewhere local, the introduction of animals could be the more sustainable approach.[20] You also need to centre your energy and capacity in this decision. Do you have the time required to manage the animals on your site?[21] Looking at the 'needs analysis' explored in the Design Process chapter could help you consider the inputs and outputs of such a decision and whether it's a good option.

» **Chickens**, if appropriately managed, benefit the soil and provide eggs for home consumption. They require less space than other animals.

» **Goats** can be helpful where brambles/shrubbery have taken over your grazing land and the intention is to bring it back to pasture, or where you want shrubs planted alongside pasture. They have a high yield of milk for their size, though they require year-round housing and must be closely monitored because they can easily obliterate your shrubbery.[22]

» **Cattle and sheep**, when used together, eat the same grass to different lengths. Therefore, you don't need to increase the size of your grazing area because they coexist amicably. You probably only want cows if you have ample space. They can produce dairy products and increase soil fertility.[23]

» **Pigs** are harder to justify on ecological grounds because they compete directly with us for food. They like what we like. Pigs are the least likely to be used in a permaculture system because the outputs rarely sufficiently feed the inputs, and they can cause severe soil compaction if left for too long.[24]

Once you have decided what species of animal you want, it is time to be specific about the breed.

Some questions to consider:

» What age do they reach sexual maturity?

» What's their diet like (and can I sustain this with waste products)?

» What housing do they require?

For example, when choosing chickens, consider that some breeds may produce eggs more regularly but are more prone to disease.

How to manage animals in a permaculture system

» **Free range** means you just let them do their thing in a contained area. This will degrade the soil and can render it barren, which is not ideal.[25]

» **Rotational grazing** is viable for sheep or chickens and requires use of a moveable fence, house or what some call a 'chicken tractor'.[26] This is beneficial because, through the breaking up of soil and depositing of organic matter, nutrition and aeration benefit soil health. You move them throughout the site to enrich the soil without depleting any single area. The timeframe of this will entirely depend on context, and a critical consideration here is your own time and energy. This requires high energy input and can be a lot of work alongside an existing busy schedule.

» **Silvopasture** refers to an area of trees in which animals can graze like pigs in apple orchards.[27] This means they eat the waste product of decaying, fallen fruit and contribute to soil health. It's a way of thinking about how to get the most out of the space you have.

So there we have it! We have reached the end of the earth care section. So far, we have explored how our hands can make a positive difference when they interface with nature. We have learned how to create a design that benefits the wider ecosystem by increasing biodiversity, improving soil health and building resilience to climate change.

Wherever you are in the design process, the earth care approach can teach us how to be with the Earth symbiotically. As we move forward, we will explore the meaning of permaculture on a personal and global level, but the attention to nature in this section should remain at the heart of our work as we expand outwards. While writing this book, I have at times felt completely lost and insecure. Whenever I feel those worries arise, I take myself to the water or I put my feet on the earth and suddenly it all falls into place, the fog dissipates and I am of the Earth again: fallible, humbled and awe-stricken. If ever you feel disconnected or find yourself straying, give yourself over to the great love in the soil sky: the vital natural world.

PEOPLE CARE

WHAT DOES PERMACULTURE MEAN TO YOU?

COLLECTIVE

NURTURING

NATURE'S COMMON SENSE

INTUITIVE

SOCIAL ECOLOGY

REPAIR
REUSE
REPURPOSE

HOPE
PURPOSE
CONNECTION

WAY OF LIFE

SELF SUSTAINING LAND

COMMUNITY

"IT MAKES SENSE"

TOGETHERNESS

CONNECTION TO NATURE

Chapter 10
Self Care

'Self-love cannot flourish in isolation'[1]

– *bell hooks*

'Wild Geese' is a poem by the renowned nature poet, Mary Oliver. I owe a great deal of my work to her; my adoration for the simplicity and savagery of nature and my belief in creative writing as a vessel for change. This piece perfectly embodies the practice of sustainable self care by inviting the reader to connect with nature, to forgive our flaws as mortal bodies and to find belonging to the family of the Earth beyond the human world. Poetry does its job best when it acts as a mirror and reflects back at us the work we ought to do, so I invite you to read and then reflect on 'Wild Geese' as you explore this chapter. In doing so, you will be able to anchor what we learn here in the wild world of imagination, creative expression and nature awe.

People care is the aspect of permaculture that defines how we care for ourselves alongside caring for the planet. It acknowledges that we are all reliant on each other and that every living entity is worthy of compassion. To enact people care, we begin with the individual. As Looby Macnamara explores in her groundbreaking book *People & Permaculture*, tending to our own needs is instrumental in becoming capable of facilitating change.[2] Macnamara refers to the inner work as investigating our own 'zone 0', the place which requires the most energy and investment and provides the necessary resources to tend to the rest of the garden.[3] This tells us that our approaches to earth care can apply to our own internal landscape and that we should work within ourselves before we can work elsewhere. People care starts here and sprawls out to our local communities and the global community to which we all belong.[4]

The design principles can help us to configure how we want to be in the world, as well as what we want to grow in our gardens. The first design principle is to **observe and interact**; whilst the process of planetary and people care is not linear, there is a reason this principle is where we begin. Observing and interacting with our inner worlds is the first step towards enacting care on a larger scale, and the invitation is to do so with curiosity instead of judgement. As we learned in the design process, we must embed ourselves wholly within a context before making adjustments suitably. It is the same approach with our self-work. To accept yourself in your fullness is a laborious, lifelong feat. Still, from this realistic observation, you can consider where to change yourself and the world beyond.

We start this work by claiming personal responsibility and being aware of both the harm and the healing we are capable of.[5] Responsibility can feel like an anchor dragging you down to the unknowable depths, like a burden too heavy to carry. You are not always expected to know the right thing to do or break your back in figuring it out, but claiming responsibility is required to accept how you contribute to the climate crisis, and to make informed decisions to alleviate this.[6] Owning our shit allows us to feel we can make a difference rather than being constantly at the whim of external forces. This does not deny the existence of those external forces, but it does ask us to consider how we respond to them. Self care is reclaiming our value outside of material worth. This sometimes looks like paying attention to the role we play in a system of oppression, moderating our consumption and putting our money in ethical places where we can.

Once we have claimed responsibility, our duty becomes to design systems of care and resilience within our internal environment. This can look like watching telly, having a wank, or putting off your to-do list. It can be massages and meditation, face masks or bubble baths. But there is no amount of chamomile and aloe vera that can nourish the unfulfilled chasm that lives inside many of us. Only through a sense of connection do we find true healing and empowerment. If we are to exemplify the sentiment that we are a species woven into a web of life, then our self care cannot be limited to spa breaks and individualistic affirmations. It must be radical community care and an integrated movement towards collective liberation.

What we may consider self care in the modern world is often whitewashed and Westernised. A Goopy Gwyneth Paltrow with her chicken broth and chia seeds has become the image we associate with wellness. This tells us that health and wellness are achieved by buying scented candles, expensive yoga mats or tantric tarot cards – rather than through spiritual practices that transcend material possessions altogether. The modern tide of whitewashed wellness is riddled with fatphobia, ableism and appropriation. Many practices we currently associate with self care, such as meditation, mindfulness, affirmation, and yoga, originate in Eastern faiths such as Hinduism and Buddhism.[7] Therefore, if we intend to engage with these spiritual practices, we must reference their sources and respect them in their wholeness.[8] The motivation behind people care is about 'meeting people's needs in sustainable ways.'[9] Thus, self practices which renew us without relying on harmful vices will be the most likely to sustain us through the treacherous terrain of this world.

You know your Gods, the soft animal of your body, what grants you tenderness, what pathways lend you forgiveness, and what deities offer you salvation. I will not attempt to write the script on connecting to the immaterial spiritual world – whatever that looks like for you. Regardless of what name we give to the spirit of life, it is ultimately communion with a higher power, with a spiritual entity beyond our ego. What is evident, though, is that spiritualism has been co-opted by a reductive individualistic paradigm. Capitalism tells us that liberation is to become a fully independent individual. People care tells us that freedom is about relinquishing ego and selfish wants for the betterment of the whole community, including the Gods in their many forms. It encourages us to distinguish our *wants* from our *needs.*[10] For example, our needs could be connection, laughter, nourishing food, clean air, and shelter. Our wants could be fast fashion fads or aeroplane tickets. In making this distinction, we acknowledge that there are ways to cater to our *needs* without relying on our *wants* – particularly if they manifest in quick fixes or hedonistic escape. We can give ourselves care without feeding the money-making machine and exploiting the Earth's finite resources, therefore enacting the principles of **use and value renewable resources** and **use small and slow solutions** within our self-care practices.

Invitation: Active Gratitude Journalling

You may have heard about gratitude journalling or practised it yourself. This is a process of writing about what you are grateful for each day, however big or small. Here are some extracts from mine:

» I am grateful for the private looks shared between me and my best friend, how I know exactly what she is saying without words

» I am grateful for falling asleep to the sound of my friends laughing

» I am grateful for the jasmine blossom outside my window and the sweet scent I smell when I sit at my desk

» I am grateful for the rain outside granting me permission to rest

This practice moves us from ***expressing*** gratitude to ***enacting*** gratitude, which is to practise reciprocity. If you feel gratitude for the succulent on your windowsill, say 'thank you' the next time you water it. If it's for the way someone made you feel, make them a card, or pick them some wildflowers. This is a way of extending gratitude through our outward actions. This is an integrated self-care activity because it focuses on your well-being whilst recognising that what nourishes you relies on a wider web of connections. To ask ourselves, ***'How do I give back'***? Is also to ask, ***'How do I give myself what I need?'*** because if you care for the community, the community cares for you.

If we define our worth by how much we can produce, how much power we can obtain, and how successful we can be, then our worth is fundamentally conditional. To tend to oneself through the ethic of people care is to view oneself as intrinsically valuable and worthy – because the planet needs our care, and we are the planet. To surrender to what is bigger ultimately recuperates and recharges you, but it does not mean losing yourself to the ether. It means that beyond what we view as ourselves, there is a web of life into which we are woven, extending unconditional love and asking that we make amends.

As bell hooks explores in her book *All About Love* – our inability to define love allows space for the harmful belief that it can coexist with abuse.[11] Hooks postulates that our lack of self-love is an extension of the environment we grew up in because we are a result of our experiences. The foundation of our home life, even if loving and safe, nevertheless existed within a capitalist worldview that profits off our sense of worthlessness.[12] A lack of self-love is instrumental to the survival of capitalism itself. Hooks claims that we innately understand how to give and receive care, but growing up in a culture of exploitation has warped what love and care look like to us.[13] People care is a necessary force in the world because it promotes love and care whilst actively unlearning the dominant narrative, which makes us feel unlovable in the first place.

Harm committed on a global scale results from an unloving culture. Of course, it is too simplistic to chart the trajectory of warmongers back to a toxic environment in their upbringing. This does not tell the entire story of the atrocities committed all over the world every day. But it's harder to imagine this much suffering existing in a world in which human beings feel they are worthy of love and are taught vital and regenerative skills for giving and receiving care. If we existed in a culture that encouraged us to love ourselves and each other sustainably, would it halt the cycle of harm? The violence done to each other and the Earth? These subjects are too immense to explore thoroughly, and would require therapy I can't afford to unpack sufficiently, but it's worth considering. If 'hurt people *hurt people*', what would happen if we built cultures within ourselves and our communities that transformed that hurt into care?

Nature connection is a form of regenerative care which does not rely on unsustainable infrastructure. To connect to nature is to connect intimately to the earth care we are doing and the purpose of *why* we are doing it. I am early on in a journey of engaging more sacredly with the Earth; I only know God through my inimitable awe at the natural world, or how I can feel inconsequential and consequential at once, the perpetual paradox of my slightness being my magnitude. I only know God in the laughter lines of loved ones or the feeling I get when my bare feet touch the grass in the early summer.

Connecting to the wild world beyond ourselves is instrumental in a self-care practice which reflects our interdependence. In his book *Lost Connections*, Johanna Hari interviews evolutionary biologist Isabel Behncke. She says, ‘Becoming depressed or anxious is a process of becoming a prisoner of your own ego, where no air from the outside can get in. But a range of scientists have shown that a common reaction to being out in the natural world is the precise opposite of this sensation – a feeling of awe. Faced with a natural landscape, you have a sense that you and your concerns are very small, and the world is very big – and that sensation can shrink the ego down to a manageable size … There’s something very deeply, animally healthy in that sensation.’[14]

Lack of connection to nature manifests in ailments in the brain, body and spirit, leading to increased stress, lack of motivation, anxiety and depression.[15] Modern science is catching up to these long-held ideas from many Indigenous cultures spanning the globe.[16] Though the culture of Indigenous groups is deeply unique to their own context, an overarching belief held by native people is that we are inextricably at one with the natural world.[17] Therefore, to disconnect from nature is to disconnect from ourselves.

Science is instrumental in informing those who are nature deprived of the peer-reviewed evidence that nature connection is necessary for our health and well-being. It articulates the profound knowledge within many of us in a language more accessible for some. But those here, scared for our futures and incredibly fond of trees, do not require statistics to explain what we already know. The cartesian approach of dissection and separatism are born from the same mindset which erased native cultures and is presently destroying the Earth, so we ought to keep that in mind when we use science as our only guide for making sense of the world. Trust your own body like you would a body of research or a body of water. If the rivers evoke a torrent of tenderness in your pent-up heart, if the decisive whip of the sparrowhawks wing delights you, if you feel grief at the sight of the wounded Earth, then follow that guidance. To trust those senses, to believe you are a body of research in action, is to return to wholeness. We are rewriting a way of being that respects our sensory experiences and emotions because those qualities will bring us home to the howling Earth.

Connecting to nature may feel like a daunting invitation. Some days I don't manage to leave my house, and trudging through the city to find a park or lake feels impossible. But there are ways I have connected to nature in surprising places. In the midst of a heart-bruised January, my friend Deia brought me lilies. Their scent penetrated the damp air, and I was reminded of sweetness and light. When I researched lilies, I discovered that they are planted in the autumn as they require a long dormant period of rest. I cried when I read that. (I was premenstrual and had just finished watching a video of a puppy spooning a baby, but still). Deia's gift highlighted that I was living through an autumn of my own and that warmth would inevitably find its way to me again. This exchange, of course, has an edge of sadness to it. It can feel unjust that we have only these brief instances to connect to nature, confined to reserves or patches of green in a cement-saturated world.

But to connect to nature in its fullness, we must honour our grief for what we have lost. When we notice the decline in butterflies as we walk in the park, when we cannot swim in our rivers because they are teeming with bacteria, and when we witness the green world increasingly colonised by concrete – we may experience a deep sense of loss. Though it can appear counter-intuitive, this loss is precisely what compels us towards change and renewal. Renewal relies on loss; we cannot make way for new cycles without the cycles before them reaching an end. Those who sustainably manage woodlands mimic the system of nature and intentionally keep deadwood in the forest to support the health of the ecosystem. As the wood decomposes, it returns its nutrients to the soil and becomes a home for up to a fifth of the species inhabiting the forest, enabling their life cycles to complete.[18]

It's in my nature as a poet to personify my interactions with the natural world; I project narratives onto the hornbeams and the hornets, the invertebrates and the ivy: stories of loss, love, forgiveness and grief. I feel a sense of relief when I can relate to the trees because it restores my faith in an ongoing culture beyond ego and power. But ultimately, it's a needless venture. Though we belong to the same Earth family, I'll never embody the stoic power of the elder trees who oversee the forest. In this instance, I find myself attuned to the woodland story more than usual; it's difficult to ignore the symbolism of a decaying log feeding the veins of the forest with life. It returns me to the spectacular sorrow of my own loss. Death is the seed from which life, and therefore love, blooms. Grief is the most monumental agony, but when I welcomed it in, I became renewed. Not necessarily *different* – I remained clumsy, insecure, my eyes were still hazel. But I became more open to love, more acquainted with acceptance, more able to receive the nectar of life with full presence. My fight for the survival of all life became more invigorated because I knew without a shadow of a doubt that I am impermanent. Death will come for us all. Our flesh will decay and nourish the berries and the mushrooms. Dan is the dead log in my forever forest. Through his loss, I learned to love because 'It is a holy thing to love what death can touch.'[19] It is our mortality that makes musicians of us, makes us urgent to jump in the unbridled ocean, makes us capable of mistakes and forgiveness; life is precious only because it will end. It is a holy thing to have known Dan and lost Dan, and though I wish for nothing more than another moment shared with him; to hold each other to the coco hues of Badu, to slow dance on a pebbled beach, to say thank you, thank you for everything, I can no longer greet him in his corporeal form. But I can greet him every day if I choose to. If I step into the world and feel my beating heart rattling my chest, the rise and fall of my breath, I can pierce through the arbitrary routine to see the potent and permanent world beyond my own body.

When we welcome grief as our teacher and guide, we foster a more genuine and loving culture because we accept both the significance and the inevitability of loss. In doing so, we open ourselves to the raw reality of the cyclical world. This is also inextricable from our climate change work. Through an awareness of our animate, mortal bodies, we remember what we are connected to and want to protect. When we are disjointed from that state constantly, we welcome numbness and distraction – two of the most restrictive and commonplace symptoms of a capitalist system.[20] We are not lifeless consumption machines; we are made of the same fabric as the manatees and the monarch butterflies. As we lose biodiversity, we lose a part of us. To connect to nature is to connect with the mistreatment of the Earth as a separate entity, a removed place full of endless resources that we pillage mindlessly and then have the audacity to expect endless abundance from. The only way to realistically move toward healthy change is by building a reciprocal and truly earnest relationship with the planet. Consider the principle: **creatively use and respond to change**.

Joanna Macy explores this in her workshop programme 'The Work That Reconnects'. This is a process that works in stages to acknowledge the challenge we face and how we can most usefully and authentically show up to this challenge. One of the phases is 'honouring our pain for the world' because in doing so 'we learn the true meaning of compassion: to "suffer with". We begin to know the immensity of our heart-mind. What had isolated us in private anguish now opens outward and delivers us into the wider reaches of our inter-existence.'[21] Through acknowledging our shared grief, we can move from a place of numbness to a place of connection, and from there, we can show up more readily to face the challenges in front of us.

So, how does all of this apply to permaculture? The process of naming our needs and seeking to meet them in sustainable ways is how we initiate a permanent culture of care. Ultimately, a regenerative self-care practice cultivates resilience against the many forces which render us stressed or depleted. When we fill up our cups in a way that revitalises us, we **catch and store the energy** that we can use when we feel depleted. This practice will vary for everyone, and the invitation I extend to you is to take ownership of that healing. Reclaim your loss, gather the shards of your sorrow like broken glass and use them to sculpt something striking. Consider it your duty to care for yourself because, through healing, we can learn and make adaptations that serve the wider ecosystem and therefore **apply self-regulation and accept feedback.** The principles of permaculture are a blueprint for how we work towards interconnected well-being, so remember to recentre them as you develop your own self-care practice. You are part of an ever-evolving ecology, and to meet your needs lovingly is to begin the process of meeting global needs lovingly.

Invitation: Staying Present and Letting Go, Nature Mandala

Mandalas have been used throughout history in various cultures. The word mandala originates from a Sanskrit word meaning circle, and is a dimensional symbol used for spiritual, emotional or psychological work.[22] Mandalas first appeared in the Hindu text Rig Veda c.1500–c.500 BCE but are considered a Buddhist practice.[23] Buddhist mandala art dates back to the first century BC and had spread to other regions like Tibet, China, Japan, and Indonesia by the fourth century.[24]

When we lost Dan, we would build mandalas, or rather 'Dandalas' because he (like anyone worth talking to) loved a good pun. We would gather natural detritus in silence and think of him. The creation invited us into the present moment as it is a devotional practice that requires attention, care and negotiation.

To create your own mandala, gather any objects which call to you: pinecone, fallen leaf, pebble. Start at the centre of the circle and build outwardly from there, adding whichever adornments you would like and always remaining in a circular formation. I invite you to stay quiet throughout this process, so that your senses and presence may guide you. When Tibetan monks create sand mandalas, they do so with spiritual reverence, and letting go of the mandala is to accept and rejoice in their impermanence.[25] I invite you to do the same with yours after you have spent some time sitting with it. I invite you to bring your grief for the world into this circle, and let it symbolise your temporary Earth life, which begins with creation and ends with surrender and acceptance. This can spur some deep reflections and emotions which will be valuable in connecting to your grief.

Chapter 11
Group Work

'The Earth is running out of energy resources, but there is a source of special energy that has scarcely been tapped. It is the power available in groups.'[1]

– Dale Hunter

This second layer of people care is concerned with how we collectivise within our local environments, operating on the belief that we can make wide-scale changes from local interventions and that people can contribute more positively to the world when their needs are met.[2] Group work is an integral component of a permanent culture because if we neglect to produce healthy ways of working together, we aren't creating an environment that can realistically sustain itself. We are living through the consequences of division and estrangement. We are carrying the burden of an individualistic culture which thrives off our inability to build sustainable relationships with either plants or people.

Group work is the foundation upon which we have evolved and survived for our entire history: through negotiation, collaboration, communication and resource sharing.[3] Similarly to the design process, group work provides a practical and restorative approach to managing relationships which benefits the ecology at large. It can appear reductive to apply a formula to human connections because they are far more nuanced and complex than the pollinators to the pollen, for example. However, particularly where we exist in groups working towards a shared goal, implementing an external structure that promotes cooperation, compassion, and care can support us in navigating this often turbulent terrain.[4] If we are actively committed to a practice that respects both people and the planet, we should consider how each endeavour can be more collective. In any situation, we should be asking ourselves the questions: how can I share space, educate and co-create?

We exist in various groups in society for any number of reasons. Maybe it's a book club, gardening group, AA meeting, toddlers' play group, activist group, or a team at work. As Benson writes in the book *Working More Creatively With Groups*, 'A group comes into being to satisfy the needs and wants of its members, and unless compelled to do so, members will only attend if their needs and expectations are met.'[5] It is crucial that we work to make group spaces feel safe, comfortable and enjoyable for attendees; otherwise they won't remain there.[6] Starting in our local spaces is the most accessible way to propagate healthy relationships. We can reimagine a collaborative culture instead of a competitive one and model this in our little worlds.

Nature is greater than us, far less concerned with its image or righteousness, and far more humble and wise than we'll ever be. We may have to pull up pervasive bindweed or cut back brambles in an earth care system, but the elements largely care for themselves once we've put them in the right place. Permaculture groups don't fracture because the garden stops producing; it's most often because human beings fall out. Some people scoff at the often laborious processes of meetings; some people don't see the relevance of strengthening relationships when they are there to plant vegetables, and some people find the processes to be too arbitrary and formulaic. Some people, some people, some people. As always, the list of why we disagree or don't like something is endless. But you're reading a permaculture book, which means you are figuring out how failures can be opportunities.

When we exist within spaces requiring communication, delegation and shared labour, some formulas allow us to conduct these actions safely and functionally. I offer information on some of these processes in the 'How to get involved' chapter. Regardless of which procedures are appropriate for your situation, there are ubiquitous approaches to group work which can create a healthy container for the group process.

Above all, group spaces must seek for members to feel heard and seen and, as far as possible, must seek to meet their needs.[7] This can be orchestrated through check-ins and check-outs at the beginning of meet-ups so people feel listened to and acknowledged, and everyone has a clearer picture of each other's mood and capacity.[8] Another strategy is establishing a group agreement at the beginning of the process, which is a set of ground rules for acceptable behaviour and 'how to work together effectively and respectfully.'[9] This benefits the group as it is a co-created agreement that doesn't rely on assumptions or the often fragile foundation of interpersonal dynamics.[10] The values we seek to facilitate in group spaces are openness, consensus and non-violence. To establish resilient and healthy communities, we must foster a culture within ourselves and our relationships that promotes these principles.

We are inseparable from all human beings on this Earth, however far away and different we may feel. If we are to commence the morning with gratitude for the bird song, if we are committed to building up the health of our soil, and if we are extending our compassion to the planet, *we must do the same for our fellow people.* It can be far more difficult to do this with humans than with the jackdaw or the willow. We can experience a wordless kinship that transcends ego or opinion when we connect with non-human nature, but when we engage with other people, we must accept that they may have starkly different viewpoints to our own because they can tell us - sometimes very loudly. With nature, we value difference, biodiversity satisfies our senses, and we feel enriched by a garden augmented by variety. Yet, in human relationships, we tend to favour those affirming our opinions and build a community based on shared beliefs. This isn't inherently wrong, but in a world so rife with division and individuality, we ought to seek to reconnect through difference, tend to our societal relationships like the bio-rich garden and extend compassion and understanding to humans in their plentiful forms.

We ought to view humans as their own holistic ecosystems, with bad bits, good bits, useful bits and not-so-useful bits. This can be tricky, especially within an inflammatory culture, where social media reduces fully-fledged people to two-dimensional versions of themselves. In this climate, it is far easier to demonise and view people as *good* or *evil.* But fortunately for us, we aren't living in biblical times, so we don't actually need to defeat some brewing evil dark force lurking in the depths. We are all capable of good and bad, we all perpetuate an exploitative system to some extent, and the evil forces we stand against require far more nuanced responses than a witch hunt by torchlight or a dagger through the heart. It demands our creativity and our collaboration. It needs us to recognise that capitalism is the vampire demon under our bed, capitalism is the waking nightmare that we are walking through. Capitalism thrives on separation; it's written in blood on its carnivorous carcass. It survives on a diet of disconnection and consumerism, pecking at our self-worth for dessert. The only way we are going to defeat it is through recognising our common ground, seeking to bond over where we agree rather than bickering over where we differ. We need to recognise that different opinions are a fundamental component of a free society, and we don't need to agree on everything in order to connect over that which matters most.

Many of us are defensive and ready to slander people for mistakes and misgivings.[11] This is fundamentally juxtaposed with the ethics of permaculture, which believes people are capable of immense change. If we look at what's ahead of us, we see a monumental upward climb. But we have to believe it can transform, or at least that people can adapt and make a difference; otherwise we wouldn't be here, deciphering the code of the solution. The goal should always be to understand before we critique, because the liberation movement requires a lot of womanpower.[12] Not everyone you disagree with will be a white supremacist climate change denier. You will likely have more in common than you think; most people love their families, like to laugh and eat food and enjoy the spring arriving after the winter. We should connect to others based on people care, empathy and respect rather than guilt, anger and shame. Shame is a powerful feeling and, much like the silver-tongued mycelial network, thrives in dark, unseen places.[13] If shame is untended it can become completely crippling, but if we feel safe from non-judgment, we are far more likely to bring our shame to light. Shame and guilt are not motivating forces, however they are commonly used strategies in environmental and social justice movements.[14] Shaming or judging people for their decisions only alienates them. We fight shame with empathy[15] – our ability to understand and relate to each other. Understanding is born from shared vulnerability, and this will not arise in an environment where people cannot vocalise their opinions and concerns without fear of being ostracised. We are here to create regenerative systems which revolt against the dominant, exploitative culture – so we can't use the same toolkit as the oppressors. We benefit the ruling class when we fight among ourselves. We have to nurture those sustainable qualities their power can't touch: respect, love, care and belief in our shared humanity beyond our differing beliefs. In doing so, we create a culture they cannot inflame or misguide.

Reflective journal questions

» What happens in my body when I engage with ideas that I don't agree with?

» What happens in my body when my opinions are validated and agreed with?

» Can I think of a time that I disagreed with someone and ended up changing my mind? If so, what allowed that to happen?

» Can I think of anyone in my life that I feel polarising feelings about, both good and bad? How do I hold this paradox?

» What role do my opinions play in my life?

Group spaces can often hold up a mirror to our shame, trigger residual feelings from childhood group or family systems, and be very revealing and confronting environments.[16] They can often feel like microcosms of society at large: familiar tensions manifest, power dynamics play out and conflict emerges.[17] The difference is that we can choose how to manage these instances within a collaborative culture.[18] If not mitigated properly, these issues can lead the group to atrophy, whereby the group dynamics inhibit the group from moving towards its goal.[19] During a module at university, I had to devise a drama performance within a group. There was an instance where I attempted to celebrate a group member and their experience in dancing and suggested that they could be in charge of the movement element of the performance. They were triggered by this suggestion as they felt pigeon-holed and inevitably, conflict arose. This was difficult for me as I was terrified of confrontation. I ended up shrinking and couldn't articulate myself or explain my intentions which meant it was tough to repair. An external facilitator helped to resolve the disagreement, and we both concluded we were projecting dynamics from previous phases of our lives onto each other, which inhibited the group process. We recognised that integral needs were unmet[20] within the group, so we worked together to create an environment where all felt heard and understood. This instance highlights how easy it is to project assumptions onto each other, react defensively and end up in conflict. The process that allowed us to move from this dispute was an investment in the group beyond our personal issues and the use of an external facilitator who could remain neutral and hold both of our emotional experiences.

The other side of that coin is synergy: the group's capacity to foster outcomes which they would not be able to achieve alone. Which is to say, *the whole is greater than the sum of its parts.* This can feel like a sense of flow whereby decisions are made with ease, labour is shared fairly and equally, and everyone values each others' contributions as much as their own.

Listening is the foundation of practising empathy and creating synergy. There is a distinction between *passive* listening and *active* listening.[21] Passive listening is akin to taking a picture of a landscape on your desktop, and active listening is the feeling of being on top of the hill with the choppy wind whipping at your ankles, the feeling of your feet on the gnarly earth, the sun cracking through the clouds like a yolk. Passive listening is a one-way form of communication, where the listener displays a lack of interest or ability to understand the speaker. This usually manifests in being distracted and not asking questions to understand better. Active listening is a process whereby the listener actively and intentionally wants to hear and understand the speaker, and does so through an embodied and inquisitive approach to receiving the words, by asking questions and showing a clear understanding of what the speaker has communicated.[22]

There are twelve blocks to listening explored in counselling, some of which are: **mind reading** (assuming that you know what someone will say); **judgement** (having negative feelings already established about the person speaking and therefore not truly listening to the content); **being right** (feeling more concerned with your point being correct than listening to what someone's saying), and **filtering** (only being receptive to some of what you hear and disregarding the rest).[23] I can see myself in some of these blocks, and the first step is to notice and acknowledge which of these we are privy to and then keep them in our awareness when we are listening. Other factors to keep in mind are how we are in our bodies.

» How are we sinking into this moment with this person?

» Through what lens are we receiving their words?

When we are embodied in our listening, we are far more likely to understand what someone is saying to us through their eye contact, open body language and asking questions when we don't understand.

Activity with a Partner: Active Listening

Taking on board what we have just explored in this chapter, sit down with a partner. Each person is given five minutes to speak about something important to them. The subject matter is completely your choice. It can seem odd and disjointed to time something like an emotional expression, but it illustrates the value of formulaic approaches in group spaces. One person speaks for the allotted time, if they go over or under by a pinch, that's fine – it just helps to keep the activity contained. The other person actively listens and does so without interrupting. Once the time is up, the listener communicates what they noticed and heard from the speaker. Spend as much time as you would like discussing what came up. Were there misunderstandings? Did the speaker feel heard or unheard? What is the difference between these experiences in the body? Once you have reflected, swap roles and go again. I encourage you to reflect on what comes up throughout this process in your journal.

Group spaces are confronting and difficult a lot of the time. We have likely all experienced this at work, in school, at home. What is clear, however, is that the group can be an invaluable resource in facilitating change beyond what we can conceive of as individuals. Groups allow us to model a collaborative culture within our immediate spaces, which counters a dominant culture of separation and competition. The principles to centre here are: **integrate rather than segregate** and **use and value diversity**. It's essential to the survival of people and nature that we learn how to reconnect, manage conflict, collaboratively make decisions, share resources, and work toward common goals even if we have opposing opinions, because it is that which will determine our ability to build a unified permanent culture, one which can withstand societal and ecological collapse.

Chapter 12
Wide-Scale People Care

'The Earth is what we all have in common.'[1]

– *Wendell Berry*

If you traced the lineage of your body back to its origins, you would find a small speck of green growing from a void. If you followed the trajectory of that green speck, you'd watch it expand into a grand oak, mangle into a shark fin, and form into the fossilised fingers of your foremothers, gathering kindling for the fire. We are no more than a speck on the surface of this shimmering world. A less cynical version of myself thinks all we need is more reminders of our earthliness, more time submerged in the roiling world to regard our honest reflections. I like to think if we found our way back to the fire, back to the tribe, back to the native nuance of our surroundings, we could be given grace and the opportunity to reform this world into something more beautiful and kind.

We have been plucked from the soil like roses and placed in a vase on the aristocrat's lavish dining table, an ornate feature in their indulgent banquet. But the thorn in our side is bleeding, our roots are suffocating, and the soil that conceived us is depleted and famished. To some extent, all of us are starved of connection and have been forcibly removed from nature and community. The thorn in our side is a distress signal to find our way back to the land. To phrase it this way implies that we should return to the times of yore when we spun yarn, carved spoons and ran around barefoot in fields of wheat. Whilst this sounds kind of romantic and fun, I also want to be able to watch Netflix and order a takeaway from time to time. Finding our way back doesn't necessarily mean moving backwards; it's a process of reconnecting ourselves to our roots and the wild heart within us bound with the natural world. Permaculture advocates for land sovereignty and intentional stewardship, and when this works from a people-care perspective, it promotes peoples' right to connect with nature.

The first step towards developing self-reliant systems is to advocate for everyone's right to connect to the land. We are deeply disconnected from nature, and this disconnection spawns our mistreatment of the Earth. If we view the land as kin – a feral and ferocious extension of our own bodies – we are more likely to defend it. In doing so, we can work to build a healthy and interpersonal relationship with the green-blue Earth. This advocacy is particularly poignant to me in the political climate of the UK currently. The vast majority of land within this country is owned by the elite and reserved for pruned grass and ornamental invasive species. It is offensive that the land we all belong to has been reduced to a status symbol rather than understood as our collective home.[2] In 2000, the Countryside & Rights of Way or CRoW Act was passed in England, which provided us with a right to roam on a mere 8% of natural spaces.[3]

This erosion of access has been exemplified recently in an attempt to ban wild camping on Dartmoor. Those gothic and expansive hills hold spiritual significance to the communities surrounding them, myself included. It was a heartbreaking attempt to gatekeep a communally beloved wild space from the public and place even more power in the hands of landowners. This case was brought forward by two landowners on the premise that camping in closed tents could not be classified as 'open air recreation', which is a ludicrous attempt at limiting people's free movement and right to connect with their environment. The claims hinged on the notion that wild camping could harm livestock or the natural environment, but no evidence supported this. On the 31st July 2023, in a historical victory, the ban was overturned.[4] The local uproar and peaceful protest to the restriction on camping contributed to this outcome. Thousands of people protested their Right to Roam on Dartmoor, eating picnics, holding hand-made signs, dancing and chanting and resisting the obscenity of it all. This fight was particularly significant because Dartmoor is the last remaining legal space for wild camping in the UK, and allowing this law to pass would mean relinquishing the only lawful access we have left.[5] Wild camping is still considered an open air activity even if the zip on your tent is done up, and people peacefully stargazing and resting isn't a threat to anyone, it turns out. Mercifully, some sanity has been salvaged. This case highlights our capacity for change when we come together, and how human beings can really make a difference when they organise and unite over shared goals. People coming together in shared rage, care and solidarity always gives me goosebumps because it reminds me that hope is not lost, that we are stronger when we stand together and that change is actually possible. The significance of this win should not be understated, of course, but it highlights that in order to reclaim our land properly we must build a movement which rejects the notion of land ownership and state control altogether. So much of our land is barricaded by the filthy rich who want their third or fourth houses to play cricket, sip their champagne flutes and laugh at poor people whilst sporting their garish top hats and monocles (or whatever super-rich people do).

The culture within this country is founded upon separation and private ownership. We have accepted the notion that the land does not belong to the people and that having access to the therapeutic properties of nature is only for people with privilege.[6] As the collective Right to Roam comments, in those areas not legally accessible to people, we are 'actively made to feel unwelcome in our own landscape and have been portrayed for centuries as a threat to the countryside'.[7] The arguments against fighting for our right to roam are that people need privacy. However, in many other countries throughout Europe, such as Norway, Sweden, Estonia and Scotland, where it is commonplace for inhabitants to roam the countryside, they have faced little backlash, and people's privacy remains uncompromised.[8] Others feel that if we opened more natural spaces to the public, they would be disrespected and covered in litter.[9] I see this as a bad-faith position.

There is a private waterfall near Cheddar Gorge, where the owners have allowed the public to visit and share the unique beauty of the place. I've never once seen it covered in rubbish. I heard about this waterfall through word of mouth and, on my first visit, followed a dropped pin on google maps and lots of directions from the locals. We walked up through a corridor of yew trees, their wide canopies cocooning us in a dense shade, then turned the corner and were immersed in light, our eyes squinting to adjust to the brightness. I love those moments when the elements strike me to a halt, and there's nothing to do except bask. We passed fields of bluebells and slender trees until we found ourselves at a gate with a sign which reads:

WE HAVE OPENED THIS TO THE PUBLIC SO
THAT YOU CAN SHARE THIS PLACE WITH US.
WE ASK THAT YOU ENJOY YOURSELF, RESPECT
THIS SPACE, AND TAKE HOME YOUR LITTER.

In the waterfall, we dunked our heads under the current before drying ourselves off and giggling with the hysterical euphoria only found when you jump into ice-cold water. To advocate for land access is to believe that if we open up natural spaces to the public and invite respect, most of us will adhere to that. We can only learn how to step more kindly on this planet if we are given the track to walk upon.

We are responsible for enabling the nonsense of gatekeeping land. This planet belongs to all of us, and until we recognise the injustice of privatising parts of it, we are participating in our own oppression.[10] The most prominent threat to the overlords is people's power, as illustrated by the success of the campaign against the ban on wild camping on Dartmoor. It is so endangering to them that England is fast becoming a totalitarian state. In 2022, the Police, Crime, Sentencing and Courts Act passed unprecedented power to an unjust police force that protects property over people, restricts our ability to protest and criminalises nomadic communities such as Irish Travellers and Romany Gypsies.[11] Those among us who seek to live autonomously to these power structures or protest against them are now at a far higher risk of incarceration due to the passing of this bill.[12]

The coronavirus pandemic exposed the cracks in this fragile system. We saw companies making record profits whilst more and more of the population were plunged into poverty,[13] we witnessed how unsustainable our food system really is,[14] and we felt the dangerous divisiveness of our political climate, with juxtaposing protests happening on a mass scale. It was a time when the world was at a surreal standstill. Many people flocked to natural spaces like never before, and moments of connection with nature and people felt like water nourishing our drought-stricken bodies. We were in a collective liminal space where the ground rules were different, and many of us were reckoning with existential questions about what we really need in our lives.

Many of us had the space to reevaluate what we *need* to live a fulfilling life: time spent outside, the support of others through times of suffering and celebration, access to necessary resources, our collective health, and self-organising community support when the government inevitably fails to meet our needs. It also showed us that we can adapt to new circumstances if our lives are on the line.[15] The climate crisis ought to be treated with the same sense of urgency since it literally concerns our entire species' survival. If we can grow our own food, practise intentional and necessary frugality, co-operate within our own structures and learn to live autonomously, then we are reducing our reliance on a harmful system.

It strikes me as deeply sad that the majority of us don't know what it's like to roam freely across our local landscapes or go to our back garden and pick salad leaves for dinner. The idea of living this way is often viewed as idealistic, something reserved for hippies who should get a real job. This is, quite honestly, absurd. How have we become so far removed from our roots that we see those who want to live closely with the land as unrealistic and even *childish*? To whom does this Earth belong? On the broadest scale, people care looks at how we establish restorative practices within the global community to liberate people and the planet from an exploitative regime. But permaculture is about locality, so we initiate this wild-scale action by utilising these principles in the vicinity we inhabit.

When Mollison and Holgrem established permaculture in the 1970s, it was in response to a world rapidly globalising, burning through fossil fuels driven by delusional greed.[16] Since then, our culture has become even more destructive, and our resources are all the more limited, so the need to find our way back is ever more urgent. It's easy to visualise permaculture in its most idealistic arrangement within the context of community living, which can take many shapes. It can manifest in eco-villages, tribal communities, nomadic societies such as Irish Travellers and Romany Gypsies, or land and housing cooperatives, among many others. This option is inaccessible for many of us; it often requires access to land, money, a community with a shared goal and a lot of hard work. And even if we take ourselves away to these quiet corners, the brutal world rages on beyond us. We cannot hide behind bramble barricades and ignore the noise outside. Further still, to 'own' land is a colonial concept that contributes to the merciless power structures we seek to free ourselves from.

But we can try to create havens that promote the possibility of shared power over hierarchical dominance. I grew up in a community context, so I know all too well the danger of idealism without practical application, the fragility of relational dynamics, and the level of commitment and humility required to live in a tight-knit community. Governmental forces intentionally restrict our ability to access land and grow our own food. Even if you have the money to buy land, there are bureaucratic barriers to planning permission and the necessity to prove that your land will be financially viable within a culture which demonises these unconventional ways of life.[17] However, despite the difficulties of creating and maintaining these communities, I have also seen their potential: the power of reclaiming our land, supporting each other through hardship and co-creating a healthier culture.

The emergence of intentional communities is pinpointed to the late 1990s, though they are largely modelled from the centuries-old living approaches of Indigenous communities worldwide. Geoph Kozeny, a renowned communitarian, spent time with over 350 communities. He defined an 'intentional community' as 'a group of people who have chosen to live together with a common purpose, working cooperatively to create a lifestyle that reflects their shared core values. The people may live together on a piece of rural land, in a suburban home, or in an urban neighbourhood, and they may share a single residence or live in a cluster of dwellings'.[18] This indicates that community living isn't reserved only for people who own their land; its principles can be enacted within innumerable living contexts.

In Judit Farkas's ethnoanthropological study of Eco-Villages in her native Hungary, she found common themes woven throughout various communities. Eco-villages are a form of intentional community that usually emerge on pieces of land co-owned by their inhabitants, and the principles of these settlements often interlock with permaculture values. They are founded on liberation from a harmful political system, healthy food access, collaborative decision-making, self-sufficiency, frugality and striving for autonomy. Their intention is to be 'detached from the umbilical cord' of the power-hungry infrastructure in the mainstream world.[19]

I spoke to three generations of women who have lived within intentional community contexts at different life phases. Hearing them speak of their experiences made me feel deeply connected to the feminine force within me. I felt I belonged to a lineage of caretakers and custodians, sprawling out in front of me like reeds in a tropical wetland, a steadfast staple of beauty and continuity. I imagined their stories like branches from a veteran tree, each reaching for different threads in the passing clouds yet connected by the same soil.

To respect the anonymity of these women, I will rename them here. The eldest lived in intentional communities in her early twenties and then again in her late thirties, and I will call her Elder Tree.

Another lived in these spaces in her mid-twenties, and I will call her The Sapling. The other, who experienced community living as a child, will be called The Seed. I choose these names because this is a permaculture book, so using trees as an analogy is pretty on-brand. I also found the image to be pertinent. Trees carry a sense of overseeing, all-knowing wisdom. They are sturdy and deeply embedded within the ecosystem. I saw these women in a similar light, each at different phases of their life cycle and yet belonging to the unifying ancestry of womanhood: an ancestry of sacrifice, deep knowledge, tenacious compassion, softness, fire, water, earth and air. I felt it necessary to centre women's voices in this conversation because although intentional communities are alternative environments, dominant patriarchal power structures remain prevalent. The feminine power inside all of us is a force of fierce tenderness – a place we all must pull from, regardless of gender identity, if we wish to build a restorative culture.

I was interested in understanding how these communities work in practice. The context I grew up in was a form of community that sought to live separately to the mainstream world, but there was no clear ethos or intention, and it wasn't particularly sustainable or earth-focused. The community contexts these women belonged to, spanning Guatemala,

Portugal and the UK, were starkly different in some aspects but were all founded on principles of intentionality, shared decision-making, self-sufficiency and sustainable earth practices. Shared procedures included feeding chickens, growing vegetables, natural building, meetings, facilitation, sharing circles and conflict management, among many others. Each community aimed to live autonomously from the external system as far as possible.

The Seed spoke from a place of wounding and had to wade through thickets of trauma to express their experience. They spoke with wisdom beyond their years and a sensitivity to the subtleties of their life, which provided such value to this conversation. Children are often overlooked or unseen within our culture, dismissed as lacking in awareness or not understanding the world for what it really is. The undercurrent of permaculture is to foresee a life of abundance for our children, and to do so without listening to them feels inauthentic. The Seed spoke of a profound sense of belonging to their natural space, and I felt a pang when listening to it. It is a rare perspective to hear, as children are increasingly detached from nature in the present day. She told me, 'I remember watching a movie called *The Fox and the Child*; I watched it when I lived there. I remember thinking – *that's me* – that's someone who is completely alone and only has a connection with the natural world to survive. And the land is the one healing thing from that time in my life. The one thing that I made friends with. And the one place I could find complete peace in the chaos of family and community dynamics.' She expressed struggles almost universal for children: feeling ignored, a lack of control over changing their circumstances, and going unseen and unacknowledged. However, these were compounded by her specific upbringing. Being home-schooled was particularly challenging because she couldn't engage with the same reality as other young people. Identity and friendship are some of the most meaningful elements of a childhood experience, and many young people growing up in alternative communities wish they had the common experiences of 'normal' young people.

This conversation spun two threads for me. The first was a sense that community living can instil a deep connection to nature within children, which can forge a lasting relationship for the rest of their time on Earth. The other was a recognition of how important the voice of children should be in building community. Beyond bestowing a healthy ecosystem upon our children, we must also consider what sort of culture we pass down to them. Communities must listen to all members, and if they fail to do so, they ultimately perpetuate the same dynamics they claim to break away from. We must ask ourselves what principles and practices we are modelling for the next generation.

When I spoke with The Sapling, she said 'I really loved that my work directly influenced my home. It felt very gratifying having my job contribute to my day-to-day well-being and that of the people I lived with instead of benefitting some corporation that I was detached from … Community living has also allowed me the opportunity to live on beautiful pieces of land that I would never have had access to on my own.' When I asked her what structural imbalances she observed regarding oppression and inequality, she stated that the same problems we observe in society are alive in these spaces: 'Communities are not utopias, and I think any issues that are present within society have the potential to seep their way in. Of course, a lot of communities have the goal of living alternatively and finding better ways to relate, but they still usually need to make money in order to survive, so capitalism rears its ugly head. Hierarchies often form naturally, even in communities that define themselves as 'non-hierarchical'. People's deep-rooted biases that have been ingrained in them since birth, including ableism and sexism, walk in with them through community gates. I would hope, although I haven't always seen it to be true, that community spaces provide the opportunity for us to look at inequality and discuss ways to combat it on a small scale so that it can get easier on a large one.' This is aligned with the premise of permaculture: the notion that what we model in our local area isn't merely escapism from an oppressive world but is, in fact, work which has the power to actively reshape it.

The Sapling spoke with a sense of clarity and wisdom. She did not strike me as someone with her head in the clouds, or at least, if she did spend her time cloud-chasing, her feet remained firmly on the earth. Whenever she spoke about her community lifestyle, it was never the earth care elements which required rethinking; it was about interpersonal dynamics and how they can often hinder the process. She said, 'it's extremely important that communities are clear on how decisions are made, as there are so many different structures out there, and it can be chaotic if this isn't well defined. I also think having a clearly stated vision and values ensuring that community members share these help things run much more smoothly. There's an infinite number of ways to organise communities, and rather than seeing any form as more successful than others, I think one major key to success is having all of your community members on the same page about how your specific community should be structured.'

When I spoke with the Elder Tree, I was blown away by the depth and breadth of her insight. I felt that I was speaking to someone who had walked the track I yearn to walk and was able to tell me where there was quicksand and poisonous berries, and where there was sunlight and meadows. I felt a sense of intergenerational communion, which isn't alive in the Western world. It was so valuable to speak to a woman older than me and see the connectedness of our experience. It also reminded me how rarely we listen to the guidance of the elders in our community.

She told me, 'every community is an opportunity for growth, regardless of whether it works out or not … However, these opportunities can be missed when we ignore any individuals' voices: Oftentimes there will be people who fall through the cracks. People will stop turning up, and you won't know why, so you miss the opportunity to understand where the group could have met their needs. And that's really sad.' Ultimately, the community spaces we inhabit must seek to meet the needs of those involved. Otherwise, the purpose of these spaces goes unfulfilled. Unmet needs will often align with disparities in privilege, failing, for example, neurodiverse or disabled group members. Community living fails at the first hurdle if it doesn't seek to hold space for those who lack space in our mainstream world.

We explored how community spaces and environmental spaces, on the whole, view the term 'sustainability', and how our perceptions can vary. The Elder Tree said, 'the tagline of my community was sustainability – for me that's really difficult – the way I view a word like sustainability is really broad, it's huge, it's *everything*.' She commented that sustainability isn't merely making environmentally conscious decisions, but also how we create sustainable relational cultures, too. She said, 'It's so multifaceted but one of the big things I've learned is that when people think they're talking the same language, they actually aren't. So, often we use words, we have different measurements for them. All words are measurements ultimately, but a different frame of reference governs the way that we perceive them. And privilege has a huge part to play in that.' Someone could understand completely differently what 'sustainability', 'accountability' or 'power' means, which is particularly difficult if you are trying to set up a mission statement or group agreement for your community.

The ethos of the community where she lived was 'inspired by a First Nations story' in which decisions made in the present moment account for the impact several generations into the future, 'so the children of all beings, not just human children. The first thing you've got to regard with that is there's a huge amount of listening, a huge amount of symbiotic relationship goes into that process, a huge amount of ancestral legacy passed down that gives you windows into how to be with nature and that process. You've got to have the humility to recognise that's impossible because we're not a tribe, we don't belong to this land, we hardly know it at all. There's not one of us who has sat within a metre of ground here and understood how the biosphere works just in this immediate area of ground. That we have the hubris to say we know what's best for it all is fucking ridiculous.' It seems important that we take ourselves truthfully as we are, and take action to reconnect, whilst recognising that we all come from a culture which has actively separated us from the natural world.

The Elder Tree seems to be someone committed to her self work, to a journey of healing, to understanding the shadowy underbelly of her psyche and meeting conflict and challenge with curiosity and care. We discussed the difficulty in establishing a cohesive protocol for the nuance of human dynamics. Structures for communication and group work can be beneficial, but we can't assume our work is done once we've implemented them. In order for relational dynamics to be worked through safely, community members must remain curious and open to learning. A word like 'sustainability' or the establishment of a 'permanent culture' must have within it principles of adaptability, humility, deep listening, willingness to receive feedback and a commitment to seeing people in their wholeness. It's ultimately not possible to write a 'how to' on ways of managing complex people, especially if they have been oppressed, exploited or traumatised throughout their life, so at the core, we must seek to listen to people and *be with* them as far as possible. She said, 'if I was ever going to join a community again, the goals would be far less grandiose. I would only want to be with people who were interested in accountability. I would like goals such as 'acceptance of what is' and 'compassion'. Before you get to the point of saying 'I want us to grow our own food', I'm interested in conversations like: are we going to look at privilege, ableism, patriarchy? Are we going to create a culture of honesty with each other?'

'I think ultimately as people we are healed by a sense of, to some degree, *safety*. As physical beings, we're never safe ... but because we're also spiritual beings – *we're always safe, and we're always enough* ... If you can let people know as far as possible that their place is secure, that they're welcome and that they are valued ... *then* you can get to the nitty-gritty of people's suffering. Uncertainty is written into our collective trauma. You can tell people countless times that they are valuable, but that doesn't mean they will hear it. You've got to ask yourself who are you in the boat with? What skills does everyone have? Get them out, have a look, nurture and support people's skills. Especially care and listening, which are often skills that women have that they don't know they have just because it's in their nature.' Above anything, if we seek to create these decentralised spaces, we must carve out space for collective joy. 'Celebration is the glue of community', the Elder Tree says. 'It needs to happen regularly, it can't be something you put off until all the work is done; it needs to be a foundational must. And that means celebration of everyone … then you know you're going to have moments of connection, that place of kindness and welcoming and joy. And that doesn't mean excluding challenging feelings, but for it to be known that this is the place of celebration. Even if it's celebrating that we've got the capacity to sit with challenges.'

Whether or not you wish to live in an intentional community, these spaces can be a source of inspiration for defying the ludicrous laws of ownership and division plaguing our Earth. They stand for collectivism, people power, access to land, food freedom, self-regulation, intentional frugality and a deep sense of respect for nature. These are qualities which we can all enact more actively in our day-to-day lives regardless of the land we live on. To gather sweet chestnuts from their pricked husks and roast them on the fire, to forage the spicy stems of wild garlic for dinner's garnish, to tend to the chickens as they tend to the soil, to know the inspiring intimacy of intergenerational care: these are profound experiences that we are intentionally deprived of. Community living offers us a model of how we can live more harmoniously on this Earth by reducing our reliance on the system which is killing the planet. We must be realistic and honest with ourselves about what is achievable and how we can move towards more intentional relationships, more connectedness with the planet, and greater self-sufficiency, without expecting ourselves to immediately unlearn the toxicity of the capitalist world. These ways of life teach us how we could walk the track on this Earth. If we do so earnestly, with a willingness to learn, with an ever-deepening commitment to connecting to the wild world, we may be able to carve out a path for our children's children to walk.

The Good Ancestor

Every day I walk a hundred years
to the hill where my great great granddaughter sits.
I carry words of blessing
and reach to touch her back.

But feeling me near she turns
sad eyed and heavy with grief
"What was it like?" she asks

Wide-Scale People Care

"when the great whales swam
when the birds sang you awake,
when the rains came soft
and the soil smelt sweet underfoot?"
And the blessings
catch in my throat.

On darker days she turns,
her famished face charred and eyes,
sunk in their bony orbits,
burn with curses.
And the blessings
froth at my mouth
with the poisonous
spume of betrayal.

On the darkest of all days
I walk the hundred years
and find no one there.

Let today be the bright day.
Let today be the bright day
I lay my hand upon her back
And, feeling me near, she turns
and blesses me, saying
"Your love was fierce enough,
sweet ancestor,
your love was fierce enough."

Daverick Leggett,
For Those Who Rise Today

How fierce is our love?

FAIR SHARE

IT FEELS NEW AND WHITE
WHEN IT IS
AS OLD AND BLACK AS THE SOIL

"FOR SOMEONE STRUGGLING
WITH CHRONIC HEALTH PROBLEMS,
THERE IS A CONSTANT PRESSURE
TO BE NOTICED FOR WHAT I DO
INSTEAD OF EVERYTHING I AM"

LACK OF CULTURAL
AWARENESS

DO YOU HAVE ANY CRITIQUES OF PERMACULTURE?

"WE SHOULD TEACH PERMACULTURE
AS PART OF OUR EDUCATION SYSTEM
– IT'S WHAT WE NEED TO
BUILD RESILIENT COMMUNITIES"

INDIGENOUS ROOTS
NOT ALWAYS ACKNOWLEDGED

DOMINATED BY WHITE
MIDDLE-CLASS PEOPLE

Chapter 13
Intersectional Permaculture

'We cannot save the planet without uplifting the voices of its people – especially those most often unheard'[1]

– *Leah Thomas*

In her short story 'The Ones Who Walk Away From Omelas', Ursula K. Le Guin writes of a world of overflowing beauty and happiness: folks dancing in the street, flowers of every colour, food of every flavour, sunshine and clear blue seas, all the delectable and joyous elements of the human experience. For this indulgence, however, the city dwellers must pay a price. They know one child, trapped and tortured, lives a life of pain and suffering to facilitate their life of luxury: 'They all know that it has to be there … they all understand that their happiness, the beauty of their city, the tenderness of their friendships, the health of their children, the wisdom of their scholars, the skill of their makers … *depend wholly on this child's abominable misery.*'[2] It doesn't take much imagination to comprehend the city Le Guin has built. We live in a world founded on rotted roots, flea-riddled foundations of colonial genocide and violence. We know that children are exploited, wildlife is extinguished, the planet's finite resources are forcibly stolen; we know that in exchange for the seemingly abundant world in which we reside, other living entities are paying the price.

The story concludes with inhabitants choosing to walk away from the city of Omelas. This is one definition of activism: refusing to partake in a world where one's freedom comes at the cost of another's persecution. I am fascinated by why we don't take this step ourselves – what forces prevent us from doing so? What makes us fear the cliff edge, the precipice? Is it the unknown? Is it the sacrifice? For some, survival and self-preservation are the only choices available. For others, the reality is too horrible so they choose to look away. The answers are different for all of us and very much sculpted by our privilege and experience of the world.

Fair share recognises that Omelas cannot be a city of opulence if it is at the expense of the suffering of living beings. It is the tenet of permaculture that focuses on equality and justice.[3] Fair share looks at how we self-regulate and live more mindfully within our own limits so that resources can be equally shared for all that inhabit the Earth. It recognises that our resources are limited and need to be shared amongst many beings.[4] Consider the principle **apply self-regulation and accept feedback.** This includes basic needs: clean air, clean water, shelter, healthcare, education and, beyond that, shared liberation and joy. Fair share a political polyculture, an embodied biodiversity that respects the eclectic and unique value of all communities, both ecological and human.

The term 'intersectional feminism' was coined by Kimberlé Crenshaw in her revolutionary text 'Demarginalizing the Intersection of Race and Sex', which brings together intersections of oppression experienced in society and unpacks how they coexist, challenging the preconceived notion that experiences of race and experiences of gender are entirely separate cultural issues.[5] She writes, 'the better we understand how identities and power work together from one context to another, the less likely our movements for change are to fracture'.[6] This is a principle echoed throughout permaculture; that the diverse connections between all beings make for a stronger system and we are far more vulnerable to threat if we neglect to value these interlocking factors. Consider **integrate rather than segregate**.

Our ability to recognise the nuance and complexity of oppression is largely indebted to the wisdom and labour of Black women. This must remain a focal point of our investigations, or it becomes a reflection of precisely the unjust world it critiques, exploiting the hard work of marginalised groups for profit. To honour intersectionality, we must bear witness to the work in its totality. In doing so we adopt an anti-colonialist lens, through which we honour the roots and context of the work we engage with, physical or ephemeral, as opposed to poaching that which fits our existing narrative and discarding the rest. One way to begin this process is to educate ourselves and share what we learn. There will be a list of resources to understand intersectionality better and hear first-hand from inimitable voices in the 'Further Reading' section of this book.

This movement was furthered by Leah Thomas, who coined the term 'intersectional environmentalism', a commentary on the intersections of environmentalism, racism and privilege and a recognition that the liberation of people is indivisible from the liberation of the planet.[7] The impact of the climate crisis is insidious and gradual, and the implications are far harsher on communities already at the sharp end of inequality.[8] It's a revolting reality to digest because it's telling us, 'if the social structure is already built for you to suffer, that means you are going to suffer more'. I don't know who signed off on the deeds for this reality, but someone should have warned them that the house is haunted and the garden is literally on fire.

Identifying factors such as race help us to make sense of the well-organised machine which oppresses every single one of us, but it doesn't tell the whole story of how capitalism is killing people and the planet. If we reduce human beings to only digestible fragments, we risk losing nuance and a sense of shared humanity beyond our categorised identities. Intersectionality benefits neo-liberalism when we use it as an oppression checklist which separates us even further, instead of a way to recognise that our experiences of persecution are interlinked. As Adolph Reed states in his work *No Politics But Class Politics*, the unifying force which binds us is the exploitation of our labour which benefits only the wealthy. Our movement towards change requires us to organise over shared threats, and this has been successful historically when working class and low-income people have come together to fight for justice.[9]

Rueanna Haynes, the senior legal adviser for Climate Analytics, says, 'In many countries, economic, environmental, and health vulnerability is also tied to the question of race – communities who have less access to different sorts of resources tend to be communities who are more easily exploited.'[10] The health impacts of climate change are more nuanced, but the lineage traces right back to the big beast of consumer capitalism and its intersection with wealth and race.[11] Black and Latinx communities in America are more likely to have toxic landfill sites placed in their neighbourhoods leading to higher rates of ill health.[12] A study measuring pollution levels in America found that 71% of Black Americans live in areas in violation of federal standards, compared with 58% of white Americans.[13] This ever-increasing growth of food deserts plagues the UK and the US, places which are considered to be affluent and developed. A food desert is characterised by inhabitants lacking access to healthful and affordable food. This often occurs within low-income neighbourhoods and is a direct result of our exploitative and unethical food system. In a 2012 USDA report, it was found that, in the US, 'neighbourhoods consisting primarily of low-income minority ethnic groups have limited access to supermarkets compared with wealthier, predominantly white neighbourhoods.'[14] In the UK 'more than a million people ... live in "food deserts" – neighbourhoods where poverty, poor public transport and a dearth of big supermarkets severely limit access to affordable fresh fruit and vegetables'.[15] Being so far removed from healthy food is the result of losing land skills, and most impacts those living in poverty, which, in turn, disproportionately affects marginalised communities, particularly BIPOC individuals.

Indigenous communities globally continue to fight for their land to be returned and for their right to care for the wider ecosystem for the benefit of the whole.[16] Native Americans have risked their lives to protect their holy homelands in the Dakota Pipeline Protests,[17] and Indigenous Hawaiian elders face legal repercussions for the protection of their sacred mountain in the Mauna Kea Protests.[18] As I write, Indigenous Brazilians are working to protect the Amazon from further deforestation, which is bearing unfathomable repercussions for the stability of our global ecosystem.

Speaking of two uncontacted people of his tribe killed by miners in 2019, Brazilian Indigenous leader and shaman of the Davi Yanomami or 'Moxihatetema' peoples, made a powerful plea: 'We, the indigenous people, are the guardians of the lungs of the Earth, the lungs of the Amazon. Everyone talks about the Amazon. So we want you to listen to us, to pay attention to me and my people.'

So why is it that when most of us visualise the environmental movement, it's yuppies buying organic broccoli at health food shops or white eco-warriors donning dreadlocks and crystals? (I feel the need to add a disclaimer that I am not shaming anyone for their choices or privilege; we are all doing what we can. Privilege does not exempt anyone from a difficult life, it just means that identifying factors like race, class or orientation don't make that life more difficult.[19]) Why is it that a movement disproportionately affecting these aforementioned communities is not reflected in its marketing? And why is it that in principle, permaculture centres the marginalised and is concerned with collective freedom, but in practice, it is dominated by privileged voices and can feel like something reserved for middle-class white people with money? I want to take the broccoli right out of Karen's hands and tell her to do something more valuable with her privilege than buying organic whole foods and tote bags. But really, it's not Karen's fault either: she's just doing her bit, and that's quite an aggressive tactic to get people on board with what you have to say.

The history of environmental activism has been whitewashed. In truth, the emergence of the environmental movement in the 1970s adopted many of the protest practices of the civil rights movement, such as sit-ins and peaceful protest,[20] yet civil rights are not considered relevant in the majority of mainstream environmental spaces. Despite communities of Latinx, Indigenous, Black, Asian and Chicano people being instrumental in the creation of the environmental justice movement, environmental protection seems to extend only to those already protected by a neoliberal world – the white middle class.[21] Something as fundamental as the survival of all human beings on Earth has been commodified and repackaged into an individualistic initiative. This is not accidental; aligning the environmental movement with whiteness allows it to shift away from its real origins. People power and the unity of all communities are the single biggest threat to the ruling class, so promoting individual action over collectivising plays right into their hands. First they colonise our internal narratives, and then they colonise our outward actions. But if we can rewrite the story with the truth of who the fight is led by and built for, we can orchestrate a movement which unites in a fight towards true justice: the liberation of *all* living beings.

Throughout this fair share section, I explore how permaculture can be activism. Before that becomes possible, though, we need to establish a pedagogy of intersectionality. This begins with representation. The voices of different races, genders, orientations and abilities ought to be woven into any courses which teach permaculture design, with an acute focus on honouring the indigenous roots of permaculture and intentionally diversifying the educators and contributors on all levels. Representation is just the surface layer of the problem, but it is a vital place to start. Consider representation as your mulch, supplying the soil with a diversity of nutrients. Over time and with consistent reapplication, the soil structure becomes stronger and more capable of growing eclectic life. The principle **use and value diversity** is applicable here.

Environmental spaces, which also extend to permaculture spaces, can feel as if they are reserved only for white, straight, able-bodied people. Even in the realm of nature connection and outdoor activities like climbing, cycling and hiking, we likely picture a slim-built white person repping a North Face puffer and shorts, with trail mix in their pocket and a smile exposing their pearl white teeth. Repainting an image imprinted on the collective conscience so vividly is a delicate process. Barriers that limit access to natural spaces for marginalised groups range from a lack of feeling represented and therefore welcomed into these environments, to genuine threats to safety, as there is an increased risk of attack for marginalised people in wild spaces.[22] Organisations like Native Women's Wilderness, Out There Adventures, Color Outside, Black Folks Camp Too, and Disabled Hikers are led by communities who are often gatekept from natural spaces, working to reframe the outdoors as a space for everyone.[23] There is no singular answer that will miraculously solve the problems that centuries of unchallenged white supremacy have created, but embodying the slow and gradual wisdom of the planet will help us to take steps towards change without giving up when we don't immediately see results, thus applying the principle **use slow and small solutions**. We can start by actively promoting inclusivity in the spaces we inhabit, shifting our own internalised perspectives by unlearning colonial ideologies and ensuring we promote intersectionality in our climate activism.

Eco-ableism is the intersection that considers how the environmental movement does not accommodate people living with disabilities and favours able-bodied people.[24] This works from the perspective of the social model of disability. This model acknowledges that our society fails to cater for disabled people, and in doing so makes 'disability' a problem for the individual, rather than a failure of our culture to hold space for the full range of human beings that live on this Earth. Ultimately, the notion of 'disability' is created by a culture which alienates those who are not able-bodied. Many facets of the environmental justice movement overlook those living with disabilities. The symbol of eco-ableism is the plastic straw, which represents practices advocated by the environmental movement failing to factor in the needs and abilities of disabled people. Many have advocated for banning plastic straws in favour of reusable or compostable materials, but disabled people may need plastic straws to drink safely and conveniently.[25]

The climate crisis is likely to cause refugee crises, a lack of resources such as food and medicine and a lack of secure housing.[26] These implications are far more alarming for individuals who require specific adaptations. Disabled people are also often among the worst affected in an emergency, with disproportionately higher mortality rates and the least access to emergency support.[27] When you couple this with the exclusion of disabled people from the environmental movement, it becomes apparent how urgently we need to adapt our strategies and hold space for disabled communities in this sphere.

It is immensely important for people to feel that they can show up for the climate movement, but unfortunately, the most visible strategies for environmental justice campaigns are inaccessible to many. Groups like Extinction Rebellion or Just Stop Oil, for example, promote direct action through protest to unite people and stand up to power.[28] This course of action can be empowering for some, but individuals from LGBTQ+ and BIPOC communities are disproportionately targeted and attacked by the police, making them more vulnerable to arrest or violence while protesting. For disabled people, having the physical capacity to attend these spaces can also be limited, especially when accessibility is not prioritised. And to return to Karen and her broccoli, being able to buy organic, sustainable products is something inaccessible to working class people, an identifying factor that often coexists at the intersection of others, like race or ability.[29] It's a wounding irony that groups disproportionately harmed by the climate crisis can feel left out of the movement that seeks to prevent it. It is a privilege in some sense – to fight for the planet – because if you are already subjugated by society, you are fighting enough of a battle already.

I have observed ableism in permaculture spaces; although we are forming an alternative approach to life, we remain influenced by the dominant narrative, which glorifies hard work and tethers a human's worth to their output. However, permaculture spaces can actively cater to the needs of those exploited by the system and provide healthy forms of activism unavailable in more visible strategies. We must use these spaces as opportunities to improve accessibility and make adjustments to accommodate the whole spectrum of human experience. This can be implemented literally in a design system by building raised beds which can aid those with less mobility to garden without bending down. We can instigate this adjustment internally too, by respecting the various ways humans bring value to an environment that aren't about ability or output. We may not all have the capacity to be out in the streets fighting for the revolution, but we can all plant seeds and watch herbs grow, we can make the world more abundant and resilient from our back garden. In carving out space for everyone, we help build a more interesting and beautiful world.

Tammi Dallastan is prolific in horticultural design and people care aspects of permaculture. She is a woman who embodies the sun and the moon; there is a resolute, watchful softness about her and a rising tenacity and warmth. She's one of those people you'd feel safe with in the apocalypse. Tammi has an endless list of contributions to the world of permaculture. She has always felt a deep love and connection with the natural world, growing her first plant aged three. After completing her PDC in 1999, she helped to set up Brighton Permaculture Trust, supported the Permaculture Association's pathway to registering the diploma with the Open College Network, and initiated Paramaethu Cymru (the Welsh permaculture network). She has run Ragmans Lane Farm, trained permaculture tutors on diversity and equality on a global scale, and is currently a trustee for the Permaculture Association and director of Field Families – a CIC that puts on permaculture areas at festivals such as Glastonbury Festival and Green Gathering.

On one of the work weekends for Glastonbury, as everyone rose from their tents and gathered by the morning fire to drink coffee, smoke cigarettes, and stretch into the day, Tammi wrote a list of jobs so that we could self-organise once we'd eventually peeled ourselves away from the fireside. I was inspired by Tammi's inclusions on the to-do list:

'Take time to connect with the land, notice what has changed seasonally, observe and reconnect'. It's something small, but it speaks to something huge: connecting to the land is equally valuable as building benches or repairing the roundhouse roof. It signifies what is rare and remarkable about permaculture spaces, what I often find hard to articulate. Connecting to the healing properties of nature and building a sustained relationship with the land – *this is the lifeblood of permaculture.* Permaculture spaces advocate that the inward shifts towards connection, patience and observation are just as critical as our outward actions of building and creating.

In permaculture, we are looking at how we embody intersectionality in our day-to-day lives. How do we hold that global understanding of the crossroads of inequalities and filter this down into incremental actions? How do we bring this knowledge back home, to ourselves, and to our local environment? We take intersectionality into our hands, literally, and ask *how do I take this learning and put it into the soil?*

The late Patrick Whitefield, author of the *Earth Care Manual* and beloved permaculture educator, defined permaculture as 'the art of designing beneficial relationships.'[30] Permaculture is rebellion in small spaces; it is resilience to climate collapse through forming connections. Intersectional permaculture recognises complexities of oppression which inhibit access to resources, particularly health-providing food. Agricultural juggernauts like the American-owned Cargill exploit land workers globally in places such as Africa and Brazil, add additives and preservatives to the products and own every stage of production from the moment the product is brought from farmers to when it ends up on our plates.[31] Global food production is owned by only four companies, which means any time we buy supermarket food, we are putting money in the hands of the hyper-wealthy.[32] Globalisation and growing corporate greed are the forces which oppress marginalised groups and poison our food. It is a privilege to be able to afford organic and pesticide-free food, and this is a direct result of a capitalist system that separates people from the process of production. There are direct links between the food we consume and our health, from auto-immune diseases to cancer.[33] Vandana Shiva, an absolutely badass eco-feminist, argues that globalisation is a direct threat to food security and a healthy ecosystem because poorer countries are exploited for their resources and land skills, and wealthier countries consume the unhealthy produce without connecting to its origins.[34] So ultimately no one wins except the billionaires, which seems to be a bit of a running theme at this point.

Intersectional permaculture is a commitment to sharing the fundamentals that allow us to survive and thrive, such as connection to nature, connection to community and easy access to nutritious and sustainable food. It calls upon us to consider how to **obtain a yield** which is restorative and fair. It is a movement which advocates for the free sharing of resources that empower people in a way which is healthy and hopeful. It seeks to bring us back to our local land whilst remaining attuned to wide-scale oppressions, which is to **design from patterns to details**. We focus on how we can make our immediate world a place of change, diversity, abundance, health and community. Intersectional permaculture is about making innovative, receptive and attuned adaptations in times of great instability and change. It is how we **creatively use and respond to change**. In recognising the harm we are enacting on the planet and marginalised communities, by sitting honestly with the realities of adversity and oppression, we can look realistically at the challenge ahead of us and **use edges and value the marginal**. At this stage, I would advise that you return to the permaculture principles and the reflections you made on them earlier in this book and consider how they apply to intersectionality, fair share and climate justice.

Chapter 14
Urban Permaculture

'Gardening is the most therapeutic and defiant act you can do, especially in the inner city. Plus you get strawberries'[1]

– *Ron Finley*

I wake whilst it's still dark, my body weighty like an anchor. I am pulling myself from the inky depths of sleep to greet the sunrise. It is the winter solstice, which honours the longest night of darkness in the year. I walk at this hour when the city is still asleep, families slowly stretching into aliveness, some birds commencing their chorus whilst others remain resting. I pass the multicoloured terraced houses, the man outside the off-licence bashing a dusty mat against a wall, and briefly lock eyes with a student in camo trousers stumbling into their house. There is something virginal in this phase of the morning, a sense that the sky is beckoning potential, that we have the chance to try things again, to do it better this time. To walk with more loving action, to respect each other better – if only we were given the canvas of a still-sleeping city. If only we weren't so busy and distracted, we could gather in the spectacle of this extended quiet and honour the everyday miracle of a waking world.

I am walking to meet my friend at the foot of The Mound, also known as the Narroways Nature Reserve, in St Werburghs, Bristol. This area was rescued from development by the local community in the late nineties. You can see so much of the city from there, so we congregate on fireworks night to watch the light pinprick the cityscape and gather when the sky is clear enough for sunset. I sat there with my first love when I was new to the city, and the silhouettes of the buildings were unfamiliar and therefore magical. This is a gentrified area of Bristol: cute cafés, extortionate rent prices, yummy mummies and an inordinate amount of oat flat whites. The mound mounts a railway and at the ankle of the hill, there is a garden and nature reserve where community groups plant and harvest vegetables.

It is late December so our breath is visible by a spool of steam uncoiling in the ebony air. The grass is shrouded in ice, sparkling and crunching beneath our feet. We are nature lovers, me and my friend, so are often in awe when we encounter the green world. But there was something especially spellbinding about this morning, a bewitching display reserved for the realm of dreams. The leaves, the grass and the knotted roots of trees were adorned with frost, urging us to step delicately, as if it was glass that could shatter any second. We knelt and sipped tea, greeting the rising of the sun with our aching bodies, our knees cold from the icy floor, our lungs tearing like a paper cut. And then, the big event: the sun makes its entrance, arriving with a wink behind the clouds. The silver of night becomes laden with gold. The ice begins to melt and steam yawns from the buildings. We are a part of this metamorphosis, slowly warming up along with everything alive on this hill, everything alive in this city. The concrete becomes animated and we are reminded of the humans behind each door, drinking their morning coffees or feeding their cats. We are reminded that we are all governed by the same primal cycles. We all sleep, we all wake, we all know the humbling beauty of the sunrise.

* * *

This place has become a sanctuary for me; little flecks of woodland surround it and sprawl out to a hill of allotments. It is a place where the city and nature meet a truce; the industrial metal of the railway is as much a part of the scenery as the communities of nettles and sorrel. When I moved from Devon, a place of green rolling hills and wild woods, I was quite the nature snob. Places like this seemed like vague mockeries of nature, of what it meant to be truly encased in a place with all senses catered to.

Now, I make a point of exchanging a smile with all the humans that gather on this hill, stroking all the dogs, learning the names of the different plants, and paying acute attention to the vertebrae of each leaf. I have learned the city as a place with a realness a rural village couldn't imitate: buzzing with humans in their many forms, cultures mish-mashing, art born from borders, music from the marginal, protest and prayer.

Invitation: Drawing Activity

Look a little closer and dig a little deeper. Regardless of where you reside, a means of connecting more intimately with your landscape comes through observing its intricate innards. This is a process of zooming into the delicacies and looking with an imaginary magnifying glass at the patterns within each incantation of nature. Take yourself on a trip through the city or the country lanes and walk with an acute eye. Trust your intuition; follow anything that calls to you. Maybe the flaking layers of bark or a fallen leaf. Gather anything that grabs your eye and is easily taken. Remember to request permission, express gratitude, and not take any more than you need. Once you have gathered your natural objects, get a piece of paper and some crayons. Place paper on top of each object and colour it in with the crayons. The patterns will be revealing themselves in different colours on your page. This is an invitation to scribble your inner child into being, to be playful and untethered. Continue this exploration for as long as you would like. A further invitation is to form a piece of art built around the patterns that have presented themselves to you and weave the imprints of nature into your work. Pay attention to what shifts with a sustained practice of looking more closely at your surroundings.

When we imagine living closely with nature, we often envision small villages, communities in the wilderness, or cute cobbled cottages with dried herbs above the hearth. It is unlikely we imagine an overcrowded city with more concrete than grass, air pollution and fast food chains. But the notion that the city is not a wild place is another way of separating us from the natural world. It creates a sense that nature is happening somewhere elsewhere, to someone else, and not within the borders of our own body. Nature deprivation is a chronic state for many, particularly those that live in the inner city, so much so that biophobia – a genuine aversion to or fear of nature – is now a diagnosable condition. This is the inversion of biophilia: the natural tendency of humans to adore nature.[2] The current generation of young people know their mobile phones better than they know their local green spaces and plant species are no longer common knowledge. Our connection to nature has been eroded as industrialism has expanded. Mental health crises, disconnection from nature, and fear of the outdoors are found more in city dwellers, particularly young people.[3] This indicates the value of introducing permaculture in the city as opposed to places already abundant in green. A city is a place where permaculture becomes enlivened and the intersections of people and planet coexist most powerfully. The city is where I learned the practice but also the meaning of permaculture, and saw it as something which can truthfully make a difference in the world, rather than something reserved for my back garden. The city is where my curiosity about the human experience and my devotion to the natural world befriended each other.

A place where this amalgamation is realised is in city allotments. During the nineteenth century, when industrial Britain was in full swing, allotments were provided to industrial labourers from poor communities so that they could have access to nutritious food.[4] I picture barefoot children rocking flat caps with charcoaled cheeks in the smutty city running to these reserves of land to tend to the soil. I imagine the plots becoming a sort of escape and haven, working at a different pace to the polluted city. Today, allotments carry the heritage of food sovereignty and contrast to industrialism.

* * *

Some months after the solstice, on a foreboding February day, I walk up Fishponds Road: it is suffocated with cars, the air thick with fumes, and the concrete almost sticky, like plastic treacle. I cross the road to Royate Hill Allotments, which is under the stewardship of the legendary Mike Feingold. Mike came to care for these allotments when they were at threat of being sold to developers, likely to build more houses, estimated to be worth around three million pounds in total. At that time, only a handful of people were using the allotment plots. Mike worked to prove that they had value for the community and took all remaining plots under his wing. He is renowned in the world of regenerative agriculture and permaculture and is, to be honest, a hero. Entire books could be written on his accomplishments and brevity is certainly not my strong suit, so I'll do my best to portray him sufficiently in the confines of this little book.

There are apple trees, vegetable beds, compost heaps, piles of rusty tools, cakes rescued from landfill, pots and pans, and piles of wood. Amongst them I see Mike in his natural form, pottering around with a Golden Virginia rolled cigarette spilling from his mouth. His hair is wild and grey and spiralling from his face. He is wearing his usual expression of deep thought and distant pondering. He is like something from the pages of a fantasy book, untamed in a way we don't encounter these days, and yet he remains distinctly of the Earth. There is nothing remotely airy or fake about him. He simply cares for the Earth with integrity and teaches others the language of this care. Or, as he so lovingly describes himself, he is a 'grumpy old git'.

Mike spent many years of his upbringing living and working on land which his father managed alongside Indigenous people in Kenya. Just before secondary school, Mike made his way to England to study, as the school in Kenya he would have attended no longer had accreditation since Kenya gained independence from British rule. Following in his father's footsteps, he was involved in various welfare rights campaigning for justice. He said 'It was right in the middle of Thatcherism, and everything you were losing. It was like hitting your head against a brick wall. I thought, I want to create something that I'd like to see.'

This is where Mike's permaculture work came to fruition, where he asked himself the question, '*What is it to be a good farmer?*' He spent many years moving between about six sites, attempting to answer this question. He speaks with a deep respect and gratitude for the indigenous farmers, who he learned a lot of his land-based skills from. He travelled between Peru and Bolivia, cyclically returning to observe how the land changed seasonally, honing his understanding of sensibly and sensitively managing land. He has travelled the far reaches of the globe, teaching these approaches to land management from England to India with the Gandhi Peace Centre. Travelling to Israel to learn rewilding and ask 'What makes the desert bloom?', and to Brazil to learn from the Indigenous people. He commented, 'Not many countries have words on their flag. In Brazil, the words are progress and order, which tells you all you need to know about the country and its treatment of tribal peoples'. He is known globally in the field of permaculture for his rewilding projects. There is something wizardly in his ability to transform desolate spaces into abundant Edens.

These days he lives a quieter life: tending to his chickens, holding community work days at his allotment and orchard, teaching on the Shift Bristol course, running the Glastonbury Permaculture Gardens and feeding the local community with supermarket leftovers that would otherwise end up in landfill. His work exemplifies the principles **produce no waste** and **obtain a yield** in action. When I asked Mike if he was proud of the exceptional work he's done, his answer was unflinchingly humble. He told me, 'I can claim I've done all these things but actually it's much more that I've connected with people doing things … I didn't do all those things on my ownsome, I was working with other people that were active and without those other people, it wouldn't have happened. It's about finding other people who are active, and in a sense, supporting them. Rather than trying to convince the world leaders that permaculture is the best thing since sliced bread.'

Mike's work illustrates the ability of permaculture in the inner city to make a real difference to the adversities of this world. The legacy of his work is proof that to tend to green spaces in a city rife with division and inequality is to build a more resilient and hopeful future. He enacts so much of what permaculture is in principle but can fail to be in practice. He feeds the local community, teaches the skills and resources to obtain food security, honours the indigenous roots of his knowledge and does so on land which he rescued from being just another block of flats in a world of industry and ever rising rent prices. He has restored soil health and faith in this small corner of the city, cultivating a resistance richer with beauty than is conceivable by the wealthy politicians.

With urban permaculture, we have the opportunity to go against the grain of urbanisation as it is traditionally known and utilise the skills we have established through the design process. It is an opportunity to use space creatively, emancipate us from the isolation of city life and centre those on the edge.[5] The principle **use edges and value the marginal** is notably useful here. Regarding permaculture design in the city, we must be creative with how we utilise the edges as there are limitations on space. This is also relevant in regards to people care and fair share, as there is the opportunity to bring marginalised communities into the centre of these projects. We can become alchemists and activists, transforming the labyrinth of concrete into a matrix of multiplicity. We can craft edible art and embolden communities to create the world of green they wish to see. We can transform concrete jungles into fruiting forests.

An example of this in practice is the Incredible Edible Network, starting in Todmorden, Yorkshire, an initiative of growing edible plants on neglected pieces of land, supported by the local council. This has expanded throughout the UK, with communities mobilising to create their own pockets of growth amongst the desolate cityscapes. 'Gardening, say the founders, makes for a kinder, more connected community.'[6] Another example is the Picasso Gardens in the city of Parma, Italy. The emergence of a 'public park' provides a place of beauty and sanctuary for city inhabitants, a much-needed respite from the rat race. As always with a permaculture project, each facet has many forms of value, so it is a project of nature connection, food security and community building.[7] What roots these gardens in the principles of permaculture is how they encourage a relational ecology, where inhabitants establish a meaningful relationship with the land through the process of supporting its development.[8] The implementation of food forests in the inner city illustrates that regardless of our status or income, something wild within us lends itself to these spaces. We can witness the healing capacity of nature even more significantly when it is in stark juxtaposition to the context it is grown within. The intersections of injustice which relate to health, well-being and food access, can be most poignantly mitigated in the inner city, where the plant life provides a healthy sanctuary for inhabitants, actively absorbs carbon emissions and mitigates climate change effects. The principle **use and value renewable resources** comes into focus here, as the medicinal and therapeutic benefits of nature can be even more valuable for people when implemented in urban environments. The image of bees buzzing, wildflowers flourishing and birds chirruping becomes even more powerful when you imagine it amongst cars and concrete.

Another example of urban gardening is the work of Ron Finley in South Los Angeles – also known as the 'Gangsta Gardener'. In his compelling TED Talk, Finley says, 'South Central Los Angeles: home of the drive-thru and the drive-bys.

Funny thing is, the drive-thrus are killing more people than the drive-bys.'[9] He has witnessed the intersections of poverty, race and health: 'I see kids of colour, they're just on this track that's designed for them, that leads them to nowhere.'[10] He wanted to change that trajectory and make his home more abundant in tomatoes and potential, so he kickstarted an initiative of local volunteers called LA Green Grounds and planted an edible forest full of vegetables and herbs on an unused plot of soil outside his house. This is guerilla gardening, where you plant something on land you don't own in an effort to resist power structures which inhibit our access to land and food,[11] and make better use of neglected spaces. This is a process of **using the edges and marginal** and **designing from patterns to details**, in which one observes the holistic vision of a system and then uses this to inform the detailed decisions. Recognising the societal structures of oppression and responding by taking small steps to change it perfectly exemplifies the value of this principle in community gardening work. His movement has grown exponentially and he has succeeded in resourcing many members of the community with the skills to feed themselves from the soil. In his signature suave tone, he says, 'to change the community you have to change the composition of the soil. And we are the soil.'[12]

Finley's work embodies so much of permaculture practice but in a different lexicon, since he is known predominantly as a guerilla gardener and hasn't used the specifics of the design process in his work. This speaks to something integral about permaculture; the practice seeks to **integrate rather than segregate** and **use and value diversity**. What is special about the language of the soil is that it transcends barriers. So, to move our hands with kindness in accordance with the cycles of nature is a practice we can all share regardless of what we call it. Language is a tool of precision; it is born from the human impulse to dissect reality and constrain it to the boundaries of the sensical. This is a useful function and one which gives us the sucker punch of poetry and the joy of conversation. It can, however, separate us from each other. Bill Mollison defined permaculture as an autonomous movement, somewhat apolitical in that it transcends any particular governing strategy.[13] This, in theory, allows it to be untouchable and accessible to anyone interested, regardless of our political leanings or backgrounds. It overlaps and is intertwined with many practices with different titles –regenerative agriculture, herbal medicine, ecology, environmental justice, therapeutic group work, arts and health, organic horticulture and community engagement, among numerous others. The permaculture design process, principles and ethics give language to what many of us view to be intuitive and sensical. Permaculture is a home for anyone who feels frustrated by the infrastructures of oppression, who is exhausted by the blind eyes turned to the climate crisis, and who wants to do something about it by transforming their local spaces. Anyone trying to build resilience, connection, and biodiversity is an ally in this movement. The most fundamental element of urban permaculture in particular is its ability to break down the boundaries that separate us and promote hope and connection in the places where it is the most vital.

Chapter 15

Restorative Activism

'If freedom means doing what I want
well that means, I've got to know what that is,
not just what it isn't.'[1]

– *Ramshackle Glory*

The parameters of permaculture as activism, or as I am defining it here, 'restorative activism', manifest in two steering forces. The first is community land work as an empowering and remedial tool. The second is the will of our imagination to bring forward the change we want to see. This chapter explores the former by looking at permaculture projects that empower communities to reclaim healing and facilitate food freedom. We will be exploring the latter through a far more intimate inquiry. This requires an excavation of our innards; it requires courage to step into a future vision of possibility and embody the shifts required to take ourselves there. Restorative activism, in essence, is the establishment of a permanent culture beyond the remit of our current experience. It is helmed by an undercurrent of stewardship, love for our future children, and compassion for our planet beyond the rewards we may gain in our brief time spent here.

We can realise some of our hopes by pouring our hearts into our own natural spaces, mobilising communities and resourcing them with skills. But for this to be truly meaningful activism that leads us towards wide-scale change, we ought to carve out space to manifest and dream. Restorative activism is literally the process of envisioning the world that we desire on the horizon and allowing ourselves to be so drenched in its brilliance that every action we put forward into the world becomes something which wills itself towards that dream.

I hope I'm not losing you with these words. What I'm saying might sound as ludicrous as suggesting unicorns live inside the minds of politicians or that Big Pharma put microchips in the covid vaccine. However, the notion that our dream of saving ourselves from destruction is a delusional portrayal of the future is a far more maddening way to face what we're up against. This view is reserved for those who have been eroded and hardened by the world, and who can blame them? This hellscape invites nihilism, but that is ultimately right where they want us. Since how we take action is led by how we frame the crises ahead of us, potentially the most radical thing we can do is dare to dream beyond the limitations placed upon us.

Restorative activism seeks to build a movement in which it's utterly sensible to dream big, to believe that the difference you make in your local space will make ripples in the wider waves of the world, to worship the earthworms, to view the waters and the soil as family, and to look for meaning in the passing clouds. If we are adopting the belief that our existence is an extension of a wider ecosystem, then the logical assumption would be that the changes we make in our little lives ultimately impact the wider ecology. It is entirely anti-establishment to think this way. Dreaming of the world on the horizon takes immense bravery, creativity and adaptability. All of the great thinkers and social justice leaders of history that pushed us towards collective change had the audacity to dream bigger than what they could see before them. Restorative activism is a way of viewing the oppressive power structure as something that has the capacity to change, as opposed to a sinking ship with no survivors. I recognise that the signs currently point towards drowning, but if that is to be inevitable, surely we want to feel that we did all we could for ourselves, for our families, for the spinning sphere we call home. Or maybe we just want to keep our heads above water long enough to know love, tenderness, laughter; that rich reservoir of experience which cannot be colonised.

The privilege of living a life of liberation and possibility should not be reserved for the wealthy. They have destroyed and stolen so much *but they cannot take away from us our will to dream.* A movement towards change must have within it the possibility of hope, otherwise, the meaning is completely lost. This also has a practical function because it is more likely to build a sustained and ongoing activism as opposed to something which burns us out to the point of paralysation. Adrienne Maree Brown explores the notion of 'pleasure activism' in her book *Pleasure Activism: The Politics of Feeling Good.* The term was originally coined by Keith Cylar, the founder of Housing Works, a not-for-profit New York-based charity combating AIDS and homelessness.[2] Brown says, 'We have to be able to feel what it is we're longing for. We have to be able to feel the light in order to keep going – in order to know that we're getting somewhere".[3] We may go through bouts of feeling disillusioned, unable to see the light at the end of the tunnel. This is a completely natural response and a part of *realistic optimism*, as opposed to the insufferable live-laugh-love, hands-over-the-ears optimism, which is produced by ignorance of the issues at hand.

Underpinning the notion of pleasure activism laid out here by Brown is the work of the utterly iconic, self-described 'black, lesbian, mother, warrior, poet'[4] Audre Lorde. My words are a butter fingered portrayal of Lorde, so I urge you desperately to read her work – you will be changed. Lorde's will to dream beyond the external world presented to her is a source of inspiration for any of us struggling to do the same. Her work teaches us how to move towards justice in a way that transcends conceivable possibility, in a way that touches the deepest and most sacred parts of ourselves and surfaces our wildness, our primal and awe-inspiring connectedness.[5]

The essays 'Poetry Is Not A Luxury' and 'Uses of the Erotic: The Erotic as Power' speak of our capacity for illumination beyond what is supposedly possible. Lorde writes that we ought to seek the effulgence of our true selves, to animate the world we want to see in our poetry, in the ways we practise passion in the wilderness of each other's bodies, in how we lead with loving action and nurture our children.[6] Lorde's power in existing authentically in her identity and embodying her queerness and blackness in a climate which polices these qualities[7] tells us that, specifically because we are oppressed by this system, seeking joy, making beauty, building connections, having orgasms, resting without pressure to produce, and making art for the sake of art are in themselves acts of radical self-love, therefore radical outward love. In the 'People Care' section of this book we explored ways to care for ourselves and each other more restoratively, and here I invite you to recognise the poignancy of such an act. Middle finger to the leaders who reduce us to profit margins. Middle finger in the wet puddle of your pleasure. We are beings of the Earth with beating hearts, with hands that touch the terrain of bark and hairs which stand in ovation in celebration of satisfaction. These are no small acts in the face of a world which works actively to repress desire, profits from our self-loathing, and seeks to eradicate any incarnation of pleasure which isn't heteronormative or hedonistic.

One way that we make activism restorative for ourselves is to be fully present in our land work. To be connected to nature and community is incredibly good for our well-being and mental health, and it keeps us returning again and again, despite the bad weather, to plant our seedlings and to share our cups of tea. When we see the land transform into different shapes and colours, we are reminded that our hands are catalysts for change because we are seeing the manifestation of our hard work right in front of us, and that is immensely valuable for our health. As Brown explores in her work, another crucial element of pleasure activism is the sharing of food.[8] There is something ancient and interconnecting about sharing food; humans have been doing it for our entire evolution, and it has sustained us through millennia. When this is woven into justice movements, it is often a moment in which people feel deeply connected to one another, and has resonance which transcends our temporary bodies. This becomes particularly meaningful in permaculture activism because food justice is instrumental in this movement. When I picture the journey of my activism: protests, protest camps, sustainability courses, permaculture builds – some of the deepest and most binding memories are sharing soup or salad or chocolate in a circle. Permaculture works towards justice by resourcing communities with Earth-healing practices which, in turn, provide them with a healthy yield of food. If this activism is to be truly restorative, then we must seek to slurp up every fragment of fructose from the flesh of the fruit and revel in the joyousness of sharing food as much as we put our hard work into growing it.

'Hope is a discipline'

– Mariame Kaba [9]

Beyond soaking up the sap of our experience, there are practical ways we can work to shift our perspective to something which is more hopeful and restorative. In their collaborative book *Active Hope: How to Face the Mess We're in with Unexpected Resilience and Creative Power*, Chris Johnstone and Joanna Macy explore how to move from a place of fear and numbness to a place of action. This is embodied horizon work because it looks at how 'hope' can be a verb – a word of action as opposed to an intangible concept.[10] Macy and Johnstone are renowned practitioners who have been in the business of enlivening hope in people all over the world for decades. They distinguish *passive* hope from *active* hope to demonstrate a shift in responsibility and power from external forces to our own internal capacity to make a difference. Active Hope is a lens through which we view the world, moving us closer to the changes we want to see. They write, 'Active Hope is a practice. Like Tai Chi or gardening, it is something we *do* rather than *have*.'[11] Active Hope is rooted in three phases: seeing the situation we are in with open eyes, identifying what we want the world to be like, and taking the steps to bring us closer to that reality. Whilst this may read like a simple step-by-step guide for something deeply challenging, this practice doesn't require us to feel full of hope or even able to cope at all times: 'Since Active Hope doesn't require our optimism, we can apply it even in areas where we feel hopeless. The guiding impetus is intention; we *choose* what we aim to bring about, act for, or express. Rather than weighing our chances and proceeding only when we feel hopeful, we focus on our intention and let it be our guide.'[12] The colossal chaos of climate change, exploitation, injustice and the global pandemic spurring even harsher wealth disparity are indicators of something Macy and Johnstone dub 'The Great Turning', which refers to the holes in the fabric of our world becoming exposed and the bruised skin beneath revealing itself. This shift in our view of reality requires us to be kind to ourselves by perceiving 'Active Hope' as something we can work at each day rather than some unattainable state, reserved for the delusional or the privileged, inaccessible in a world of so much cruelty and suffering. It asks, 'Taking in the reality of what's happening in our world, what's the best we can hope for? And how can we be active in making that more likely or even possible?'[13]

Permaculture can promote a permanent culture in activist spaces and thus transform them into something far more sustaining and beneficial. Rosemary Marrow established the project Permaculture for Refugees, travelling around the world with this organisation throughout Bangladesh, Italy, Greece and other places where refugee settlements exist.[14] This initiative intended to rework and regenerate some of the harmful cultures of temporary refugee sites.[15] This is starkly different to the 'white saviour' approach, whereby organisations implant themselves in places without listening to the voices of the people they are supposed to be 'rescuing'. Though the people who established Permaculture for Refugees did so from a place of privilege, the enterprise is decentralised and person-led by the refugees themselves, working to actively detangle the top-down approach refugee camps are founded upon.[16] The camps are created to be temporary but often end up remaining there for years, so a long-standing culture is established on the shaky foundations of a 'temporary' set-up.[17] Marrow says 'For camp residents and local communities, they are negative spaces – often overcrowded ... built on powerlessness and disconnection, with poor infrastructure and sanitation ... camps can degenerate into shanty towns or squalid slums with internal conflicts. Flow-on effects include the spread of infectious diseases, fear and mistrust.'[18]

Permaculture is an approach which fully embeds itself in the needs of a context and then takes action to make that context healthier for all living beings within it. The power of such initiatives is that they promote self-sufficiency and longevity, whereby the skills and education acquired remain long after they have been taught. Permaculture is innately hopeful and seeks to view problems as potential opportunities for change – it is not defeatist or fatalistic. Whilst the governmental approach to the refugee crisis is deeply unethical and dehumanising, there are areas of land set aside for these communities, which is a resource that can be utilised.[19]

Restorative activism goes beyond demanding change from the global power structures. It recognises that we cannot negotiate with an obscenely unethical system and we will not change anything by cooperating with our oppressors. Permaculture gets its hands dirty and works at shifting cultures from unhealthy to regenerative from the inside. Since Permaculture for Refugees started, their work has had profoundly positive effects on refugee camps worldwide. Through implementing cooperative group work structures, a cooperative culture seeped out 'from the classroom to the implementation of projects'.[20] Immediate change could be seen in better waste awareness, healthier cohabitation with less conflict, easier decision making and creative design approaches.[21] The longer-term effects saw Permaculture Design Courses being taught by refugees for refugees and NGOs adopting strategies from the perspective of a more permanent culture as opposed to a temporary one.[22] A transformative element of establishing a continuous culture is the hope that it can promote for individuals living in these spaces.[23] After experiencing deep trauma and displacement, feeling resourced to adapt to unpredictable circumstances beyond their current situation was a notably empowering experience for residents, facilitated by permaculture principles.[24] Marrow commented, 'As well as enabling positive change within the camps themselves, permaculture can be a source of hope for the future.'[25]

Applying this approach to other activist spaces can also be beneficial. For example, protest camps such as those set up in resistance to HS2 in the UK are temporary camps created by activists as they risk their safety on the frontlines to protect people and the planet from injustice: in this case, protecting an ancient woodland from a planned high-speed railway.[26] This is incredibly brave and important work, and I have witnessed remarkable resilience within these communities of people. What I have also seen, however, is the light in people's pupils snuffed out, and their bodies waning over time. I've seen people whose care for the inequities of the world eat them alive from the inside. Protest camps often manifest similarly to refugee camps in that they are temporary infrastructures subject to turbulence, so it's difficult to create consistency and cohesion amongst so much instability. Add in an extra dollop of police and state violence, damp and cold and you have a recipe for conflict and burnout. In these cases, the principles of permaculture can offer respite and regeneration, even on a small scale. Shifting our frame of thinking to be more permanent and established can have a monumental impact, because even if the space itself is temporary, we can carry the culture forward, restoring our faith in our ability to make lasting change. We desperately need that faith in order to keep going.

Simple implementations such as sustainable waste management, catching and storing readily available water and making use of waste products can be implemented almost immediately when temporary protest camps are set up. Beyond that, the approaches of group work can be instrumental in spaces like these for the activists to work collaboratively towards a shared goal where people feel heard, and conflict can be mitigated in a healthy way. This is also a way of preparing us for what is likely ahead in our lifetimes or the lifetimes of our children. The climate crisis will see an increase in refugee migration, natural disasters and a lack of access to services and resources, so learning how to utilise community bonds and create restorative practices within temporary setups is ultimately climate change resilience. It's an opportunity to aid ourselves in the fight ahead in a way which advocates for a hopeful outlook, even in the midst of deep grief and uncertainty.

Permaculture also becomes a source of restorative activism through the process of mutual aid. This is an act of community care whereby those belonging to any particular movement or space extend resources and support to each other separately to governing bodies, often due to organisations lacking the ability to provide us with what we need.[27] This can happen in myriad ways, from deep listening to seed swaps; from sharing anarchist literature to community mental health support. Mutual aid places the power back in our hands rather than those of top-down charity organisations that perpetuate capitalist power structures more than they break away from them.

An example of mutual aid that uses nature's healing capacity is the work of radical herbalists. The organisation Herbalists Without Borders[28] exemplifies how herbal medicine can, quite literally, soothe the lesions of injustice. HWB is a not-for-profit organisation which seeks to provide 'holistic care to communities and countries in need impacted by natural disasters, violent conflicts, poverty, trauma and other access barriers to health and wellness.'[29]

Nicole Rose, who founded Solidarity Apothecary, materially supports the health and wellness of those impacted harshly by state violence, poverty and climate change[30] and supports revolutionaries who fight for justice and are mistreated by a deeply harmful and inhumane prison system.[31] Their work is abolitionist and empowers individuals to restore themselves with herbal medicines.[32] They have written a handbook for the incarcerated on how to harness the healing within the food and herbs available in this context, as well as guides on how to manage and mitigate burnout.[33] To picture a dandelion growing in the dark corners of a prison cell is to recognise our capacity to blossom even in the most limiting contexts. To view ourselves as belonging to the same family as the plants that can heal us is the epitome of restorative activism, where plants and people work together to fight for liberation and heal their mutual wounds.

Restorative activism is for people who want to take change into their own hands and build a better world. When bound together, the ethics of permaculture (earth care, people care and fair share) forge a path for environmental justice that moves us towards change without depleting ourselves. We are given full permission to seek joy because that joy is governed by principles in direct opposition to the organised exploitation that landed us here. Permaculture advocates for defiant hope informed by the reality in front of us: hope as a verb, hope as a form of resistance, hope as a lifeline. Allowing ourselves to feel good isn't a denial of the challenges we face, but a realistic way of sustaining ourselves through a complex and ongoing quest towards liberation. We recognise the lineage of injustice, we are committed to change and community healing, we deeply respect nature as the omnipotent provider of our every need, we stand in solidarity with all living beings of this Earth and *we believe that we can make impossibly beautiful things happen.*

I don't want to be somebody screaming about my misfortune while the sky is on fire. I want to catch the flames and use them to cook dinner, to feed the bellies of the people hungry for freedom. Permaculture is just one strategy of activism, and it asks us how we show up for this crisis with care every day of our lives. We are invited to consistently rise to the occasion of this harrowing loss and greet it with those evergreen elements of attention, listening, humility and curiosity. Permaculture is about walking the walk lovingly, which means we lead with the world that we want to see. If we are angry at the capitalist system, are we countering their methods of division and disconnection by building sustainable relationships with plants and people? If we care for the planet and want to make a difference, are we intentional with what we consume and where we place our energy? If we genuinely want things to change, are we practising that change within ourselves? If we are baffled by the absurd mindlessness of pillaging a finite Earth to the irreversible point of our own extinction, are we creating sensible and healthy alternatives to that reality? Do we have a fathomable imagining of what this world could be like if we manage to topple the oppressive structures? Are we practising the possibility of what we envision, what we deserve, in all domains of our lives? Restorative activism is a way to embody change authentically.

It's really bleak out there, and we're all trying our best. So be kind to your tender heart and know that to make beauty in the face of so much horror is an astonishing act. Now give yourself a biscuit. You've earned it.

Invitation: Creative Writing Activity

In Audre Lorde's legendary essay 'Poetry is Not a Luxury',[34] she urges the reader to illuminate the world they envision through the written word. She tells us that we can bring our dreams to the light, those dreams we feel in our bodies but do not yet have a clear vision of, through our poetry. Or, more pertinently, she tells us that poetry is that light itself. So the invitation is to craft that light, to bring forward the illumination of your wildest dreams in the hope that it might help those dreams to become reality.

What world do you dream of on the horizon?

This is an opportunity to dream big, to bring the world you dream of into the light through the power of your words. You can free-write, which is a process of writing freely without editing yourself; use excerpts of anything you find inspiring as a template; or you can weave together quotes that build this world of hope. To give you a starting point, the first line of this piece can be 'The world on the horizon is...'

If words are not your forte, you can draw it, dance it, cook it. However you manifest it, I urge you to take some time basking in the possibility of it. I urge you to belong to it. Even if it's makeshift and temporary, allow yourself to be hopeful and clumsy and human. Grant yourself permission to dream.

Epilogue (The World on the Horizon Is...)

The world on the horizon is righteous with gold. I know the algae by name, I speak the language of lichen, and when I lie down in the tall grass, I know I am with kin. Where there once was concrete, there is soil: asphodel overwhelms the asphalt, vines climb the brick and cement. At night, we gather on our doorsteps and sing wonky ditties to the night sky. The stars are no longer muted by the lifeless glare of shop windows and offices. The mornings are rich with wrens and warblers, adorning the dawn with their song. The waters are healthy, and when the day is humid and oppressive, we swim with the dragonflies and river eels. Just yesterday I saw an otter cleaning her silky fur by the river bank, and it was not a miracle. I saw many winged creatures flirting with the water's surface, and it was not a miracle. When I am hungry or in need of healing, I take myself to the garden. Just *the* garden, not *my* garden, because the garden is everyone's garden. When a loved one dies, we kiss them on their cheeks, we ornate them with cowslip and place moss at their feet to protect them on their journey to the unknowable *onwards.* They grow into apples or lemon balm, and we eat their blossoming bodies. In doing so, we accept that we are temporary and infinite because loss itself renews us. Dan is immortalised in the characters of the garden; I recognise his twiddling thumbs in the knuckles of the oak tree, his golden curls in the unfurling of the fern. I am reminded of his untainted tenderness in the laughter of the children who play here. Always we lead with love, always with gratitude, and always the trees are greeted as family. When someone is hurt by someone else, we gather in a circle and we listen. We do not hide behind curtains of phones and soulless finger-pointing. We have worked tirelessly to untangle the binds of our wounding, so we seek to understand before we critique because we know that when one life suffers, we all do. Our worth is not defined by our output but instead by how we facilitate a supportive ecology, how we practise deep listening and dance the ancient waltz of reciprocity. The climate crisis is a cautionary tale from another life. And we are humbled by our interdependence, our respect for all life, our ability to adapt and heal, our devotion to the spirit of the Earth, to the spirits of each other, because that is what landed us here, holding each other clumsily beneath a smirking half moon, savouring one more second of the balmy evening before we greet the murky underworld of sleep.

How to Get Involved

Diagrams

The diagrams in this book were created by Ruby Scott-Geddes, who is a nature-loving multidisciplinary artist living in Bristol. They facilitate drawing and foraging workshops and life drawing classes alongside creating their own nature-rich print-based art. You can engage with and support their work by following them on Instagram at @ruby.makes.art or via their Linktree at linktr.ee/rscottgeddes.

How to support indigenous communities

Find out what Indigenous land you live on

» Native-Land.ca

» Whose.Land

Organisations to support

» Cultural Survival

» International Work Group for Indigenous Affairs

» Survival International

» Minority Rights Group International

» Native American's Rights Fund, Australian Institute of Aboriginal and Torres Strait Islander Studies

» Native Women's Wilderness

Indigenous Activist History

» Dakota Access Pipeline Protests

» Mauna Kea Protests

» Occupation of Alcatraz

Further reading

Indigenous literature

- Bruce Pascoe, *Dark Emu*
- Shawn Wilson, *Research Is Ceremony: Indigenous Research Methods*
- Lyla June, *Lifting Hearts Off the Ground: Declaring Indigenous Rights in Poetry*
- Robin Wall Kimmerer, *Braiding Sweetgrass*

Intersectionality literature

- Kimberlé Crenshaw, *On Intersectionality*
- Leah Thomas, *Intersectional Environmentalist*
- Audre Lorde – *Sister Outsider*, 'The Master's Tools will Never Dismantle The Master's House'
- bell hooks – *All About Love, Feminist Theory From Margin to Centre*
- Adolph Reed – *No Politics But Class Politics*

Permaculture literature

- *Permaculture Magazine*
- Patrick Whitefield – *Earth Care Manual*
- Rosemary Marrow – *Earth Restorer's Guide to Permaculture*
- Bill Mollison – *Permaculture Principles & Pathways Beyond Sustainability – A Designers' Manual*
- Looby Macnamara – *People & Permaculture* [Macnamara holds PDC's and transformative workshops on her smallholding named Applewood Permaculture Centre. More info at: applewoodcourses.com]

- L. Alderslowe, G. Amus & D.A. Devapriya – Earth Care, People Care and Fair Share in Education

Restorative Activism Literature

- Chris Johnstone and Joanna Macy – Active Hope: How to Face the Mess We're in with Unexpected Resilience & Creative Power
- Rose June, Solidarity Apothecary – The Prisoners Herbal
- Permaculture For Refugees – Full PDF available at permacultureforrefugees.org
- Adrienne Maree Brown – Pleasure Activism: The Politics of Feeling Good

Group Work

Consensus Decision Making

- Seeds For Change, or more info at consensusdecisionmaking.org

Non-Violent Communication

- The Center For Nonviolent Communication

Active Hope more info & training

- Activehope.info
- Resilience training: Chris Johnstone: chrisjohnstone.info
- Collaborative meeting strategies: Seeds For Change PDF: seedsforchange.org.uk/handsig.pdf
- The Work That Reconnects: joannamacy.net
- Clementine Morrigan – Fuck The Police Means We Don't Act Like Cops to Eachother

Permaculture design course

The best way to get involved with permaculture is to attend a Permaculture Design Course. If you are in the UK or Europe, heading to the Permaculture Association website and searching their course guide 'Section 1' will help you to locate a PDC in your area. If you are in the South West of England, I strongly recommend the Shift Bristol year-long Practical Sustainability Course, which is where I fell in love with permaculture. If you are in America or Canada, you can find PDCs through the Permaculture Institute, Earth Activist Training, or the Permaculture Institute of North America. Google is your friend if you're looking to find something close to where you are!

Transition towns

As explored earlier in this book, we need to enter into a phase of energy descent rather than energy growth.[1] Transition Town Totnes is a grassroots community group. This group's goals are to reduce energy consumption and boost the local economy, alongside building resilience to the impacts of climate change.[2] Anyone can get involved and develop skills by connecting with communities that share passions and goals. The network has now grown to a global scale, and you can find any existing groups near you via Transition Network.[3]

Connecting to communities

Whilst there are downsides to the increased use of social media, it does enable us to connect to groups of people far more easily. If you use platforms like Facebook, a quick search for local gardening groups, permaculture groups, or allotment groups can lead to meeting people who share your interests and finding the work that you want to do with others. This can be useful if you would like to share skills or hold work days on your land. Connecting with these groups online means you can inform people of these events and build networks of community whilst you build your system. If you want to get some hands-on experience, often permaculture projects will offer room, board and skill sharing in exchange for your time and energy. Organisations such as 'Permaculture Global' connect permaculture groups worldwide. You can also look for land projects through the Permaculture Association.

Guerilla gardening

If the activist in you is compelled to do some of your own guerilla planting or gardening, visit GuerillaGardening.org. This can inform you with top tips and connect you to community events.

Or: read the groundbreaking book by Ellen Miles, *Get Guerilla Gardening: A Handbook For Planting in Public Places.*

Seed swaps

Seed swaps are a way for gardeners to share seeds and promote access to food without needing to pay money. It is a form of radical mutual aid and community care and could lead to forming long-standing connections in your local area. Which is very permaculture!

» UK – London Freedom Seed Bank, Stroud Community Seed Bank

» Europe – Community Seed Banks Academy

» North America – Organic Seed Reliance

» Canada – The Bauta Family on Canadian Seed Security

No-dig

No-dig gardening was explored in the 'Soil' chapter of this book, and more in depth information can be found on Charles Dowding's website or youtube page at: charlesdowding.co.uk

Inspiring Organisations

» The Permaculture Association

» Permaculture Women

» Children in Permaculture

» Herbalists Without Borders

» The Landworkers Alliance

» The Rewild Project

» Foraging groups near you via Eat The Planet

How to Get Involved

- Ecovillages / communities via EcoVillages Worldwide or Global EcoVillage Network
- The Soil Association
- Ron Finley Foundation
- Land In Our Names
- Out On The Land
- Wolves Lane
- Ecological Land Coop

Bibliography

David Holmgren. *Essence of permaculture*. E-book, Mellidora. 2001

Kevin Morel, Francois Leger and Rafter Sass Ferguson. *Permaculture. Encyclopedia of Ecology*, 2nd edition, 4, Elsevier. 2019.

Permaculture Principles, permacultureprinciples.com/permaculture-principles. Accessed 2023.

Patrick Whitefield. *The Earth Care Manual: A Permaculture Handbook for Britain and Other Temperate Climates*. Permanent Publications. 2005.

Robin Wall Kimmerer. *Braiding Sweetgrass: Indigenous Wisdom, Scientific Knowledge and the Teaching of Plants*. Penguin. 2013.

Looby Macnamara. *People and Permaculture: Designing personal, collective and planetary well-being*. Permanent Publications. 2013.

Leah Thomas. *The Intersectional Environmentalist: How to Dismantle Systems of Oppression to Protect People + Planet*. Voracious, Hachette Book Group. 2022.

Endnotes

Prologue

1. Jean Shinoda Bolen MD. *Goddesses in Everywoman: Powerful Archetypes in Women's Lives.* HarperCollins. 2004.
2. David Holmgren. *Essence of permaculture.* E-book, Mellidora. 2001.
3. D. Holmgren, Ibid.
4. George Monbiot, 'The trespass trap: this new law could make us strangers in our own land.' *The Guardian,* 2020, theguardian.com.
5. 'Who owns the UK?' *ABC Finance Limited,* 2022, abcfinance.co.uk/blog/who-owns-the-uk.

Chapter 2: What Is Permaculture?

1. Richard E. Porter, Larry A. Samovar, Edwin R. McDaniel. *Communication Between Cultures.* Wadsworth. 1991.
2. Bill Mollison and David Holmgren, *Permaculture One: A Perennial Agriculture for Human Settlements.* Tagari. 1978.
3. Bill Mollison and David Holmgren, *Permaculture Two: Practical Design for Town and Country in Permanent Agriculture.* Tagari. 1996
4. Rohini Walker, 'The Indigenous Science of Permaculture', *PBS SoCal,* 2019, pbssocal.org/shows/tending-nature/the-indigenous-science-of-permaculture.
5. Kevin Morel, Francois Leger and Rafter Sass Ferguson. *Permaculture. Encyclopedia of Ecology,* 2nd edition, 4, Elsevier. 2019.
6. Kevin Morel, Francois Leger and Rafter Sass Ferguson. Ibid.
7. Bill Mollison and David Holmgren, *Permaculture Two: Practical Design for Town and Country in Permanent Agriculture.* Tagari. 1996
8. 'Permaculture Ethics'. *Permaculture Principles.* permacultureprinciples.com/ethics. Accessed 2023.

9. R. Walker. Ibid.
10. Shawn Wilson. 'What is an Indigenous research methodology?' *Canadian Journal of Native Education*. Vol. 25, Issue 2. 2001. pp.175-179.
11. S. Wilson. Ibid.
12. Bruce Pascoe. *Dark Emu*. Scribe Publications. 2018.
13. Lyla June. '*3000-year-old solutions to modern problems*'. *YouTube*, uploaded by TEDx Talks. 2022. youtube.com/watch?v=eH5zJxQETl4.
14. 'Plants as People Care'. *The Permaculture Podcast*. Scott Mann. 2023.
15. 'Decolonisation'. *Oxford Learner's Dictionary*. oxfordlearnersdictionaries.com/definition/english/decolonization. Accessed 2023.
16. Chenae Bullock. 'Decolonizing Our Relationships With Each Other and Mother Earth'. *Cultural Survival*. 2021. www.culturalsurvival.org/publications.
17. The Permaculture Podcast. Ibid.
18. Melinda Hinkson. 'Refiguring the postcolonial for precarious times: introduction'. *Postcolonial Studies*. Vol. 23, Iss. 4. 2020. pp.431-437.
19. 'Plants as People Care'. *The Permaculture Podcast*, Scott Mann, 2023.
20. 'The 5 Best Free Apps To Help Identify Plants'. *The BackYard Pros*, thebackyardpros.com/best-free-apps-to-help-identify-plants. Accessed 2023.
21. *Inaturalist*, www.inaturalist.org. Accessed 2023.
22. 'Publications'. *Fields Studies Council*, field-studies-council.org. Accessed 2023.
23. Robin Harford. 'Top Plant Identification Books For Foragers', *Eatweeds*, 2020, eatweeds.co.uk/plant-identification-books.
24. *CornellLab: Merlin*, merlin.allaboutbirds.org. Accessed 2023.

Endnotes

Chapter 3: Why Is it Important?

1. 'UN climate report: It's 'now or never' to limit global warming to 1.5 degrees.' *United Nations*, 2022, un.org/en/climatechange.
2. '5 Alarming Facts about Climate Change.' *UN Office for Parnerships*, 2022, unpartnerships.un.org.
3. Tim Gore. 'Confronting Carbon Inequality.' *Oxfam*, 2020, oxfam.org/en/research/confronting-carbon-inequality.
4. Karen McVeigh. 'West accused of 'climate hypocrisy' as emissions dwarf those of poor countries.' *The Guardian*, 2022, theguardian.com.
5. Chris Harris. 'Why recycling is not the answer for fighting the plastic pollution problem.' *Euronews*, 2018 euronews.com.
6. 'Greenwash.' *Cambridge Dictionary*, dictionary.cambridge.org/dictionary/english/greenwash. Accessed 2023.
7. Christopher J. Rhodes. 'Permaculture: regenerative – not merely sustainable.' *Science Progress*. Vol. 98(4). 2015. pp. 403–412.
8. Kevin Morel, Francois Leger and Rafter Sass Ferguson. *Permaculture. Encyclopedia of Ecology*, 2nd edition, 4, Elsevier. 2019.
9. Kevin Morel, Francois Leger and Rafter Sass Ferguson. Ibid.
10. Susan Clayton.. 'Climate anxiety: Psychological responses to climate change.' *Journal of Anxiety Disorders*. Volume 74. 2020
11. S. Clayton. Ibid.
12. Johann Hari. *Lost connections: Why You're Depressed and How to Find Hope*. Bloomsbury. 2018.
13. J. Hari. Ibid.
14. J. Hari. Ibid.
15. Tom Hirons. 'Sometimes a Wild God', *Tom Hirons*, 2017, tomhirons.com/poetry/sometimes-a-wild-god.

Chapter 4: The Twelve Design Principles

1. 'Principle 1: Observe and Interact.' *Permaculture Principles*, permacultureprinciples.com/permaculture-principles. Accessed 2023.
2. 'Principle 2: Catch and store energy.' *Permaculture Principles*, permacultureprinciples.com/permaculture-principles. Accessed 2023.
3. David Holmgren. *Essence of permaculture*. E-book, Mellidora, 2001.
4. D. Holmgren. Ibid.
5. D. Holmgren. Ibid.
6. 'Principle 3: Obtain a yield.' *Permaculture Principles*, permacultureprinciples.com/permaculture-principles. Accessed 2023.
7. 'Principle 4: Apply self-regulation and accept feedback.' *Permaculture Principles*, permacultureprinciples.com/permaculture-principles. Accessed 2023.
8. D. Holmgren. Ibid.
9. 'Principle 4: Apply self-regulation and accept feedback.' *Permaculture Principles*, permacultureprinciples.com/permaculture-principles. Accessed 2023.
10. 'Principle 5: Use and value renewable resources.' *Permaculture Principles*, permacultureprinciples.com/permaculture-principles. Accessed 2023.
11. D. Holmgren. Ibid.
12. D. Holmgren. Ibid.
13. 'Principle 6: Produce No Waste.' *Permaculture Principles*. permacultureprinciples.com/permaculture-principles. Accessed 2023
14. Bill Mollison. *Permaculture: A Designers Manual*. Tagari. 1988.
15. 'Principle 7: Design from patterns and details.' *Permaculture Principles*, permacultureprinciples.com/permaculture-principles. Accessed 2023
16. 'Principle 7: Design from patterns and details.' *Permaculture Principles*, permacultureprinciples.com/

permaculture-principles. Accessed 2023.

17. 'Principle 8: Integrate rather than segregate'. *Permaculture Principles*, permacultureprinciples.com/ permaculture-principles. Accessed 2023.
18. D. Holmgren. Ibid.
19. Deb Hirt. 'The Raven and the Wolf: A Study in Symbiosis.' *Owlification*, 2023, https://owlcation.com/ stem/The-Raven-and-the-Wolf-A-Study-in-Symbiosis.
20. 'Principle 9: Use Slow and Small solutions.' *Permaculture Principles*, permacultureprinciples.com/permaculture-principles. Accessed 2023.
21. D. Holmgren. Ibid.
22. D. Holmgren. Ibid.
23. 'Principle 10: Use and Value Diversity.' *Permaculture Principles.* permacultureprinciples.com/ permaculture-principles. Accessed 2023.
24. D. Holmgren. Ibid.
25. D. Holmgren. Ibid.
26. D. Holmgren. Ibid.
27. 'Principle 11: Use edges and value the marginal.' *Permaculture Principles*, permacultureprinciples.com/ permaculture-principles. Accessed 2023.
28. E. Patrick Johnson. *Appropriating Blackness: Performance and the Politics of Authenticity.* Duke University Press. 2003.
29. D. Holmgren. Ibid.
30. 'Principle 12: Creatively use and respond to change.' *Permaculture Principles*, permacultureprinciples.com/ permaculture-principles. Accessed 2023.
31. D. Holmgren. Ibid.

Chapter 5: The Design Process

1. *Shift Bristol*, shiftbristol.org.uk. Accessed 2023.
2. Patrick Whitefield. *The Earth Care Manual: A Permaculture Handbook for Britain and Other Temperate Climates.* Permanent Publications. 2005.

3. *'How to find contour maps for AutoCAD.' Community Heritage Maps, 2023, communityheritagemaps.com/how-to-find-contour-maps-for-autocad.*
4. *SunCalc*, suncalc.org. Accessed 2023.
5. 'Permaculture Design Principles'. *Permaculture Principles*, permacultureprinciples.com/permaculture-principles. Accessed 2023.
6. Elizabeth Waddington. 'Understanding Sectors in Permaculture Design'. *Permaculture Plants*, permaculturеplants.com/sector-analysis. Accessed 2023.
7. 'Zoning'. *Permaculture Association*. permaculture.org.uk/design-methods/zoning.
8. *Permaculture Association*. Ibid.
9. P. Whitefield. Ibid.
10. P. Whitefield. Ibid.
11. Adapted from Patrick Whitefield. *The Earth Care Manual: A Permaculture Handbook for Britain and Other Temperate Climates*. Permanent Publications. 2005. Artwork by Ruby Scott-Geddes.
12. P. Whitefield. Ibid.
13. P. Whitefield. Ibid.
14. P. Whitefield. Ibid.
15. *Permaculture Principles*. Ibid.
16. P. Whitefield. Ibid.
17. P. Whitefield. Ibid.
18. *Permaculture Principles*. Ibid.

Chapter 6: Soil

1. Wendell Berry. *The Unsettling of America: Culture & Agriculture*. Counterpoint . 2004. p. 70.
2. 'Top 10 Interesting Facts About Soil.' *QuickCrop, 2014,* www.quickcrop.co.uk/blog/top-10-interesting-facts-about-soil .
3. Environment Agency. *The state of the environment: soil.*

2019. www.gov.uk/government/publications/state-of-the-environment/summary-state-of-the-environment-soil.

4. Environment Agency. Ibid.
5. Environment Agency. Ibid.
6. Elizabeth Murphy. *Building Soil: A Down-to-Earth Approach: Natural Solutions for Better Gardens and Yard.* Cool Springs Press. 2015.
7. E. Murphy. Ibid.
8. 'Mason Jar Soil Test'. *PreparednessMama,* 2021, preparednessmama.com/jar-soil-test.
9. E. Murphy. Ibid.
10. Diagram adapted from: 'Mason Jar Soil Test'. *PreparednessMama,* 2021, preparednessmama.com/jar-soil-test. Artwork by Ruby Scott-Geddes.
11. *PreparednessMama.* Ibid.
12. *PreparednessMama.* Ibid.
13. *PreparednessMama.* Ibid.
14. *PreparednessMama.* Ibid.
15. Patrick Whitefield. *The Earth Care Manual: A Permaculture Handbook for Britain and Other Temperate Climates.* Permanent Publications. 2005.
16. P. Whitefield. Ibid.
17. P. Whitefield. Ibid.
18. P. Whitefield. Ibid.
19. P. Whitefield. Ibid.
20. P. Whitefield. Ibid.
21. P. Whitefield. Ibid.
22. P. Whitefield. Ibid.
23. *Permaculture Principles,* permacultureprinciples.com/permaculture-principles. Accessed 2023.
24. P. Whitefield. Ibid.
25. P. Whitefield. Ibid.
26. P. Whitefield. Ibid.

27. '*Green Manure Crops: Planting and Management Tips.*' EOS Data Analytics, 2021, eos.com/blog/green-manure.

28. P. Whitefield. Ibid.

Chapter 7: Water

1. 'How Many Countries Don't Have Clean Water?' *Lifewater,* 2020, lifewater.org/blog/how-many-countries-dont-have-clean-water-top-10-list-and-facts.
2. Sandra Laville. 'Shocking state of English rivers revealed as all of them fail pollution tests'. *The Guardian,* 2020, www.theguardian.com.
3. Patrick Whitefield. *The Earth Care Manual: A Permaculture Handbook for Britain and Other Temperate Climates.* Permanent Publications. 2005.
4. P. Whitefield. Ibid.
5. P. Whitefield. Ibid.
6. P. Whitefield. Ibid.
7. P. Whitefield. Ibid.
8. P. Whitefield. Ibid.
9. P. Whitefield. Ibid.
10. P. Whitefield. Ibid.
11. '5 Alarming Facts about Climate Change.' *UN Office for Parnerships,* 2022, unpartnerships.un.org/news/2022/5-alarming-facts-about-climate-change.
12. P. Whitefield. Ibid.
13. P. Whitefield. Ibid.
14. P. Whitefield. Ibid.
15. P. Whitefield. Ibid.
16. P. Whitefield. Ibid.
17. 'Story'. *FelaKuti,* felakuti.com/gb/story. Accessed 2023.
18. 'Water No Get Enemy'. *Econation,* 2022, econation.one/blog/water-no-get-enemy.
19. *Econation,* Ibid.

Chapter 8: Plants

1. Alyssa Premo. 'The Connection of the Pack'. *OSU WordPress*, 2020, blogs.oregonstate.edu.
2. Patrick Whitefield. *The Earth Care Manual: A Permaculture Handbook for Britain and Other Temperate Climates.* Permanent Publications. 2005.
3. P. Whitefield. Ibid.
4. Robin Wall Kimmerer. *Braiding Sweetgrass: Indigenous Wisdom, Scientific Knowledge and the Teaching of Plants.* Penguin. 2013.
5. Heather Rhoades. 'A Three Sisters Garden – Beans, Corns & Squash.' *Gardening Know How*, 2021, gardeningknowhow.com/special/children/a-three-sisters-garden.
6. H. Rhoades. Ibid.
7. H. Rhoades. Ibid.
8. Max Ehrmann. *The Desiderata of Happiness.* Souvenir Press. 1927.
9. P. Whitefield. Ibid.
10. P. Whitefield. Ibid.
11. P. Whitefield. Ibid.
12. P. Whitefield. Ibid.
13. Matt Dunwell. 'Bill Mollison'. *The Guardian*, 2016, theguardian.com.
14. P. Whitefield. Ibid.
15. P. Whitefield. Ibid.
16. Norman. 'Cabbage White Butterfly Life Cycle.' Eden's Garden. 2020. gardenofedengardencenter.com/cabbage-white-butterfly-life-cycle.
17. Norman. Ibid.
18. Norman. Ibid.
19. P. Whitefield. Ibid.
20. 'Crop Rotation Monitoring.' *EOS Data Analytics*, eos.com/industries/agriculture/crop-rotation. Accessed 2023.

21. 'Easy Crop Rotations for Your Garden.' *Deep Green Permaculture*, 2015, deepgreenpermaculture.com/2015/05/08/easy-crop-rotation-for-your-garden.
22. 'Value of crop rotation in nitrogen management', I*owa State University Extension and Outreach*, crops.extension.iastate.edu/encyclopedia.
23. 'Crop Rotation as a method of disease control.' *Farm Progress*, 2010, *f*armprogress.com/management/crop-rotation-as-a-method-of-disease-control.
24. Charles L. Mohler and Sue Ellen Johnson. 'Managing Plant Diseases with Crop Rotation.' *SARE*, 2009, sare.org/wp-content/uploads/Crop-Rotation-on-Organic-Farms.pdf.
25. 'Forest Gardens.' *Permaculture Association*, permaculture.org.uk/practical-solutions/forest-gardens. Accessed 2023.
26. *Permaculture Association*. Ibid.
27. P. Whitefield. Ibid.
28. P. Whitefield. Ibid.
29. *Permaculture Association*. Ibid.
30. P. Whitefield. Ibid.
31. P. Whitefield. Ibid.
32. P. Whitefield. Ibid.
33. P. Whitefield. Ibid.
34. P. Whitefield. Ibid.
35. Michael Jeffrey Balick and Paul Alan Cox. *Plants, People and Culture: The Science of Ethnobotany*. Garland Science. 2020.

Chapter 9: Animals

1. Oliver Milman. 'Meat accounts for nearly 60% of all greenhouse gases from food production, study finds.' *The Guardian*, theguardian.com/environment.
2. Robin Wall Kimmerer. *Braiding Sweetgrass: Indigenous Wisdom, Scientific Knowledge and the Teaching of Plants*. Penguin. 2013.

3. R. Kimmerer. Ibid.
4. R. Kimmerer. Ibid.
5. Patrick Whitefield. *The Earth Care Manual: A Permaculture Handbook for Britain and Other Temperate Climates.* Permanent Publications. 2005.
6. P. Whitefield. Ibid.
7. 'Meat Has a Place in Culture and Tradition.' *Encyclopedia of Opinion*, 2020, encyclopedia-of-opinion.org/a/meat-place-culture-tradition.
8. Lyla June. '*3000-year-old solutions to modern problems*.' *YouTube*, uploaded by TEDx Talks. 2022, youtube.com/watch?v=eH5zJxQETl4.
9. P. Whitefield. Ibid.
10. P. Whitefield. Ibid.
11. P. Whitefield. Ibid.
12. Ross. 'How to move silently: Fox walking.' Just Stealth, 2020, juststealth.com/fox-walking-and-moving-silently.
13. Erik Assadourian. '*Fox Walking: A Natural Walking Meditation*.' Gaian Way, 2020, gaianism.org/fox-walking-a-natural-walking-meditation/.
14. E. Assadourian. Ibid.
15. E. Assadourian. Ibid.
16. E. Assadourian. Ibid.
17. E. Assadourian. Ibid.
18. E. Assadourian. Ibid.
19. E. Assadourian. Ibid.
20. P. Whitefield. Ibid.
21. P. Whitefield. Ibid.
22. P. Whitefield. Ibid.
23. P. Whitefield. Ibid.
24. P. Whitefield. Ibid.
25. P. Whitefield. Ibid.
26. P. Whitefield. Ibid.
27. P. Whitefield. Ibid.

People Care illustration

Artwork by Ruby Scott-Geddes.

Chapter 10: Self Care

1. bell hooks. *All About Love.* William Morrow. 2000.
2. Looby Macnamara. *People and Permaculture: Designing personal, collective and planetary well-being.* Permanent Publications. 2013.
3. L. Macnamara. Ibid.
4. 'People Care.' *Permaculture Principles.* permacultureprinciples.com/ethics/people-care. Accessed 2023.
5. *Permaculture Principles.* Ibid.
6. L. Macnamara. Ibid.
7. Ananya Pandey. 'The Contemporary Whitewashing of Wellness and Spirituality.' *ONEUL ZINE*, theoneulzine.com. Accessed 2023.
8. A. Pandey. Ibid.
9. L. Macnamara. Ibid.
10. L. Macnamara. Ibid.
11. b. hooks. Ibid.
12. b. hooks. Ibid.
13. Hooks, B., Ibid.
14. Johann Hari. *Lost connections: Why You're Depressed and How to Find Hope.* Bloomsbury. 2018.
15. J. Hari. Ibid.
16. Lucy Jones. *Losing Eden.* Penguin Random House. 2020.
17. Shawn Wilson. 'What is an Indigenous research methodology?' *Canadian Journal of Native Education.* Vol. 25, Issue 2. 2001. pp.175-179.
18. Jonathan Humphrey, Alan Stevenson, Phil Whitfield, Janet Swailes. *Life in the Deadwood.* Forest Enterprise. 2022.
19. Francis Weller. *The Wild Edge of Sorrow: Rituals of Renewal and the Sacred Work of Grief.* North Atlantic

Books. 2015.

20. F. Weller. Ibid.

21. 'Honouring Our Pain For The World.' *Deep Times Journal*, https://journal.workthatreconnects.org/honoring/ Accessed 2023.

22. Joshua J. Mark. 'Mandalas.' *World History Encyclopedia*, 2020, www.worldhistory.org/mandala.

23. J. Mark. Ibid.

24. Lindsey Matthews. 'What is a Mandala? The meaning and history of this highly spiritual symbol', 2022, yourtango.com/self/what-is-mandala-history-symbolism-uses-spiritual-symbol.

25. Consecrea, (2023). *The Art of the Fleeting:* Tibetan Buddhist Monks and Sand Mandalas, (online).

Chapter 11: Group Work

1. Dr. Dale Hunter. *The Art of Facilitation: the essentials for leading great meetings and creating group synergy.* 2nd ed. Jossey-Bass. 2007.

2. 'People Care.' *Permaculture Principles.* permaculture-principles.com/ethics/people-care. Accessed 2023.

3. Yuval Noah Harari. *Sapiens.* Harper. 2015.

4. D. Hunter. Ibid.

5. Jarlath Benson. *Working More Creatively With Groups.* 2nd ed. Routledge. 2001.

6. J. Benson. Ibid.

7. J. Benson. Ibid.

8. D. Hunter. Ibid.

9. 'Group Agreements for workshops and meetings.' *Seeds For Change*, www.seedsforchange.org.uk/groupagree. Accessed 2023.

10. *Seeds For Change.* Ibid.

11. Clementine Morrigan. *Fuck the Police Means We Don't Act Like Cops to Each Other.* 2020.

12. C. Morrigan. Ibid.

13. Lynn Okura. 'Brene Brown On Shame: 'It Cannot Survive Empathy'. *Huffington Post*, 2013, huffpost.com/entry/brene-brown-shame_n_3807115.
14. C. Morrigan, Ibid.
15. L Okura. Ibid.
16. J. Benson. Ibid.
17. Michele Doyle and Mark Smith. *Born and Bred? Leadership, heart and informal education.* YMCA George Williams College.1999.
18. M. Doyle and M. Smith. Ibid.
19. Looby Macnamara. *People and Permaculture: Designing personal, collective and planetary well-being.* Permanent Publications. 2013.
20. J. Benson. Ibid.
21. Joanna Pantazi. 'The 12 Blocks to Active Listening.' *Youniverse, 2019,* youniversetherapy.com/post/the-12-blocks-to-active-listening.
22. Patricia Mulvania. 'The Importance of Active Listening.' *Gift of Life Institute,* 2020, giftoflifeinstitute.org/the-importance-of-active-listening.
23. J. Pantazi. Ibid.

Chapter 12: Wide-Scale People Care

1. Wendell Berry. *The Unsettling of America: Culture & Agriculture.* Counterpoint. 2004.
2. Nick Hayes. *The Book of Trespass: Crossing The Lines that Divide Us.* Bloomsbury. 2020.
3. N. Hayes. Ibid.
4. Charlotte Elton. 'English protestors win the right to wild camp in Dartmoor. Where in Europe is it still legal?' *Euronews,* 2023, euronews.com.
5. C. Elton. Ibid.
6. N. Hayes. Ibid.
7. *Right To Roam,* righttoroam.org.uk. Accessed 2023.
8. *Right To Roam.* Ibid.

9. *Right To Roam.* Ibid.
10. N. Hayes. Ibid.
11. *Kill The Bill,* killthebill.org.uk. Accessed 2023
12. *Kill The Bill.* Ibid.
13. Molly Kinder, Katie Bach and Laura Stateler. 'Profits and the pandemic: As shareholder wealth soared, workers were left behind.' *Brookings.* 2022, brookings.edu.
14. Mario Lubetkin. '2021 Revealed The Fragility of Food Systems' *reliefweb,* 2021, reliefweb.int/report/world/2021-revealed-fragility-food-systems.
15. R. Strand, Z. Kovacic, S. Funtowicz, L. Benini, A. Jesus. 'COVID-19: Lessons For Sustainability?' *European Environment Agency,* 2022, eea.europa.eu/publications/covid-19-lessons-for-sustainability
16. Bill Mollison and David Holmgren, *Permaculture One: A Perennial Agriculture for Human Settlements.* Tagari. 1978.
17. 'A guide to buying land in the UK.' *resi,* 2020, resi.co.uk/advice/new-builds/buying-land-uk.
18. 'Who is Geoph Kozeny?' *The Transition,* thetransition.org/who_is_geoph_kozeny. Accessed 2023.
19. Judit Farkas. ''Very Little Heroes': History and Roots of the Eco-Village Movement.' *Acta Ethnographica Hungarica.* 62(1). 2017. pp. 69-87.

Fair Share Illustration

Answers gathered from attendees at Glastonbury Permaculture Gardens, online public surveys, and current and previous members of the Shift Bristol Course. Artwork by Ruby Scott-Geddes.

Chapter 13: Intersectional Permaculture

1. Leah Thomas. *The Intersectional Environmentalist: How to Dismantle Systems of Oppression to Protect People + Planet.* Voracious, Hachette Book Group. 2022.

2. Ursula K. Le Guin. *The Ones Who Walk Away From Omelas.* Harper Perennial. 2017. First published 1973.
3. Kevin Morel, Francoìs Leger, Rafter Sass Ferguson. *Permaculture. Encyclopedia of Ecology,* 2nd edition, 4, Elsevier, 2019.
4. 'Fair Share.' *Permaculture Association,* permaculture.org.uk/ethics/fair-share. Accessed 2023.
5. Kimberlé Crenshaw. 'Demarginalizing the Intersection of Race and Sex: A Black Feminist Critique of Antidiscrimination Doctrine, Feminist Theory and Antiracist Politics.' *University of Chicago Legal Forum,* Vol. 1989, Article 8. 1989. pp. 139-167
6. Kimberlé Crenshaw. 'Why intersectionality can't wait.' *The Washington Post,* 2015, washingtonpost.com
7. L. Thomas. Ibid.
8. L. Thomas. Ibid.
9. Michael Powell. 'A Black Marxist Scholar Wanted to Talk About Race. It Ignited a Fury.' *New York Times,* 2020, nytimes.com/2020/08/14/us/adolph-reed-controversy.
10. Joe McCarthy. 'Why is Climate Justice a Racial Justive Issue?' *Global Citizen,* 2021, globalcitizen.org/en/content/why-is-climate-change-a-racial-justice-issue.
11. L. Thomas. Ibid.
12. L. Thomas. Ibid.
13. Katie Valentine. 'The White Washing of the Environmental Movement.' *Grist,* 2013, grist.org/climate-energy/the-whitewashing-of-the-environmental-movement.
14. Jessica Caporuscio. 'What are food deserts, and how do they impact health?' *Medical News Today,* 2020, medicalnewstoday.com/articles/318630.
15. Patrick Butler. 'More than a million UK residents live in 'food deserts', says study.' *The Guardian,* 2018, theguardian.com.
16. L. Thomas. Ibid.

17. Sam Levin. 'Dakota Access pipeline protests: UN group investigates human rights abuses.' *The Guardian*, 2016, theguardian.com.

18. Megan Moseley. 'The Hawaiian elders awaiting Trial for protesting the world's largest Telescope.' *The Guardian*, 2022, www.theguardian.com.

19. L. Thomas. Ibid.

20. L. Thomas. Ibid.

21. L. Thomas. Ibid.

22. Heather Greenwood Davis. '9 Ways to Make the Outdoors more Inclusive.' *Outside*, 2021, outsideonline.com/culture/essays-culture/inclusivity-outdoors-adventure-world-ideas.

24. Catrina Randall. 'Eco-ableism and the Climate Movement' *Friends of Earth Scotland*, 2021, foe.scot/eco-ableism-and-the-climate-movement.

25. C. Randall. Ibid.

26. '5 Alarming Facts about Climate Change.' *UN Office for Parnerships*, 2022, unpartnerships.un.org.

27. C. Randall. Ibid.

28. C. Randall. Ibid.

29. L. Thomas. Ibid.

30. 'Social Permaculture - What Is It?' *Foundation for Intentional Community*, 2016, ic.org/social-permaculture-what-is-it.

31. L. Jordan, A. Ross, E. Howard, A. Heal, A. Wasley, P. Thomas and A. Milliken. 'Cargill: the company feeding the world by helping destroy the planet.' *Unearthed Greenpeace*, 2020, unearthed.greenpeace.org.

32. L. Jordan, A. Ross, E. Howard, A. Heal, A. Wasley, P. Thomas and A. Milliken. Ibid.

33. Sara Mostafalou and Mohammad Abdollahi. 'Pesticides and human chronic diseases: evidences, mechanisms, and perspectives.' *Toxicology and Applied Pharmacology*, Volume 268, Issue 2. 2013. pp.157-177.

34. 'Vandana Shiva on Why The Food We Eat Matters.' *BBC*, 2021, bbc.com/travel.

Chapter 14: Urban Permaculture

1. Ron Finley. 'A guerilla gardener in South Central LA | Ron Finley.' *Youtube*. Uploaded by TED. youtube.com/watch?v=EzZzZ_qpZ4w
2. 'BioPhilia.' *PsychologyToday*, psychologytoday.com/gb/basics/biophilia. Accessed 2023.
3. Jo Birch, Clare Rishbeth, Sarah R. Payne. 'Nature doesn't judge you – how urban nature supports young people's mental health and well-being in a diverse UK city.' *Health & Place*, Volume 62. 2020.
4. 'A Brief History of Allotments.' *The National Allotment Society*, nsalg.org.uk/allotment-info/brief-history-of-allotments. Accessed 2023.
5. Dirk Witte. 'Urban Permaculture - The Ultimate Guide.' *New Life on Homestead*, 2021, www.newlifeonahomestead.com/urban-permaculture.
6. 'The Guardian View on Guerrilla Gardening – Go Forth And Grow.' *The Guardian*, 2022, theguardian.com.
7. 'Picasso Food Forest.' *Permaculture Global*, permacultureglobal.org/projects/2261-picasso-food-forest. Accessed 2023.
8. Francesca Riolo. 'The social and environmental value of public urban food forests: The case study of the Picasso Food Forest in Parma, Italy.' *Urban Forestry & Urban Greening*, Volume 45, 2019.
9. R. Finley. Ibid.
10. R. Finley. Ibid.
11. R. Finley. Ibid.
12. R. Finley. Ibid.
13. Kevin Morel, Francois Leger, Rafter Sass Ferguson. *Permaculture. Encyclopedia of Ecology*, 2nd edition, 4, Elsevier, 2019.

Chapter 15: Restorative Activism

1. Ramshackle Glory. 'We Are All Compost in Training'. *Live the Dream*. 2011.
2. Adrienne Maree Brown and Emma Bracy. 'Pleasure Activism: A Feel-Good Approach to Changing the World.' *Repeller*, 2019, repeller.com/what-is-pleasure-activism/
3. Adrienne Maree Brown. *Pleasure Activism: The Politics of Feeling Good*. AK Press. 2019.
4. 'Audre Lorde' *Poetry Foundation*, poetryfoundation.org/poets/audre-lorde. Accessed 2023.
5. Audre Lorde. *Sister Outsider*. Penguin Classics. 1984.
6. A. Lorde. Ibid.
7. A. Lorde. Ibid.
8. A.M. Brown. Ibid.
9. Mariame Kaba. 'Hope is A Discipline feat. Mariame Kaba.' *Beyond Prisons Podcast*. 2018, beyond-prisons.com/home/hope-is-a-discipline-feat-mariame-kaba.
10. J. Macy and C. Johnston. *Active Hope: How to Face the Mess We're in with Unexpected Resilience and Creative Power*. New World Library. 2012.
11. J. Macy and C. Johnston. Ibid.
12. J. Macy and C. Johnston. Ibid.
13. J. Macy and C. Johnston. Ibid.
14. Charlotte Ashwanden. 'Permaculture and Refugees part 1.' *Permaculture News*, 2019, permaculturenews.org.
15. Ruth Harvey. 'Bringing Permaculture to Refugee Camps.' *Permaculture for Refugees*, 2020, permacultureforrefugees.org
16. R. Harvey. Ibid.
17. R. Harvey. Ibid.
18. R. Harvey. Ibid.
19. C. Ashwanden. Ibid.

20. 'Impact of the First PDC's in Refugee Camps.' *Permaculture For Refugees*, 2022, permacultureforrefugees.org.
21. *Permaculture For Refugees.* Ibid.
22. *Permaculture For Refugees.* Ibid.
23. C. Ashwanden. Ibid.
24. C. Ashwanden. Ibid.
25. *Permaculture For Refugees.* Ibid.
26. 'Ancient Woodland Protection Camps.' *HS2 Rebellion*, www.hs2rebellion.earth. Accessed 2023.
27. 'What is Mutual Aid?' *Solidarity Economy Association*, solidarityeconomy.coop. Accessed 2022.
28. *Herbalists Without Borders*, hwbglobal.org. Accessed 2023.
29. *Herbalists Without Borders.* Ibid.
30. 'About.' *The Solidarity Apothecary – Herbal Medicine As Mutual Aid*, solidarityapothecary.org. Accessed 2023.
31. *The Solidarity Apothecary.* Ibid.
32. *The Solidarity Apothecary.* Ibid.
33. *The Solidarity Apothecary.* Ibid.
34. A. Lorde. Ibid.

How to Get Involved

1. *Transition Town Totnes*, transitiontowntotnes.org. Accessed 2023.
2. Transition Town Totnes, Ibid.
3. *Transition Network*, transitionnetwork.org. Accessed 2023.

Acknowledgments

Thank you to Christina Knight for your contagious laugh, the depth of your heart and your humble guidance.

Thank you to Ruby Scott-Geddes for your unparalleled kindness, creativity and groundedness.

Thank you to Mike Feingold, Tammi Dallaston, the gang at Glastonbury Permaculture Gardens, my Shiftie family and everyone else who shared some of their stories with me – it honestly means the world.

Thank you to the Permaculture Association for being the most informative and reliable resource in the UK bringing together our collective learning about permaculture. Its influence, and that of my course at Shift Bristol, can be seen throughout the pages of this book.

Thank you to Craig Larkin, Valentina Coccarrelli and Miles Ford – for your love, laughter, support and bouquets of flowers.

Thank you to Oscar Turner for your guidance in the early imaginings of this book.

Thank you to my beloved Trillz, Hugh, Sophie Alyce, Em, Alex, Danny, Louis, my Rooted family, and my astounding community of friends. Platonic love is the best!!

Thank you to my mum, for teaching me resilience and loving me so fiercely and without condition.

Thank you to the River Avon, the London Planes of St Andrews Park, the stoic Heron of Eastville Lake, the Kingfisher I met in Snuff Mills, the woodland sparrows and the city crows.

Thank you to Sarah Pugh and Dan Sterling for teaching me life's most valuable lessons in this realm and the next.

Thank you to Rosie Hilton, for your mutual love of Beyoncé, your hard work and profound insight – your edits made this book so much more impactful.

Thank you to the artists who shaped me and were featured in this book. To Tom Hirons, for his poem 'Sometimes A Wild God', which has been with me since I was a naive teenager who believed I could change the world. Thank you to Daverick Leggett for his poem 'The Good Ancestor', which perfectly symbolises permaculture as a movement which fights to feed our future children. And thank you to Ramshackle Glory; a disbanded folk punk band who made one of my favourite albums in the world, and gave voice to my rage, guilt, hypocrisy and joy for the broken world. Thank you specifically to Pat The Bunny, whose songwriting is incomparable and has forever changed me. Art is not needless or futile, it gives voice to the parts of us which feel voiceless, and that shit matters.

And to Deia Burdis, for everything.